MASTERBUILT ELECTRIC SMOKER COOKBOOK

150 FAST, EASY AND DELICIOUS RECIPES FOR YOUR WHOLE FAMILY AND GET-TOGETHER WITH 1000-DAY MEAL PLAN

D1738148

ALAN DERULO

TABLE OF CONTENTS

DESCRIPTION

For many years, smoking food was a necessity—hunters needed a way to preserve whatever parts of the animal couldn't be consumed immediately—and the delicious taste imparted by smoking was just a bonus. But as society moved away from the hunter-gatherer model (became more "civilized"), smoked foods gradually became prized, even coveted, for their taste. Before refrigeration, the only way a diner who lived far inland could enjoy seafood was in its smoked or dried form. But even smoked foods had to be moved great distances, adding transportation costs to the final price, which is how smoked oysters became a luxury item available only to the wealthy few.

Masterbuilt Electric smokers are some of the company's most popular products. They are a mainstay on "Best Of" lists and boast great reviews on sites like Amazon. How do Masterbuilt electric smokers work, exactly? In all smokers, a heat source cooks the food and causes wood to smoke, imparting the flavor of the wood into meat or vegetables. In an electric smoker, that heat source comes from a metal rod heated by electricity. Wood is put above the heating element where it smolders, creating smoke. To control the temperature of the heating element, you use a controller pad that lets you adjust the temperature, time, and other features your smoker might come with.

This guide has the most delicious masterbuilt electric smoker recipes perfect for any occasion. Grab this copy and enjoy the recipes inside.

Happy cooking!!

INTRODUCTION

So, you have an electric smoker and after reading the walkthroughs, you're very excited about using it. There are some other tools you should think about having, however, before you really dive in. Must-haves like quality grilling gloves, a meat thermometer, and a smoker cover keep smoking safe, convenient, and enjoyable:

BBQ gloves

Smokers are hot. To protect yourself, invest in a good pair of heat-resistant gloves. Expect to pay between $15 and $30. Try on a pair before buying, so you can see how well they grip tongs and fit on your hands.

A Meat Thermometer

You need to know the internal temp of your meat, so a meat thermometer is a must. There's a variety to choose from, but a lot of people like the wireless ones. This lets you check the temp of the meat without opening the smoker and losing heat. The range on most wireless units is about 100-300 feet. If you're buying a digital electric smoker, we would also suggest getting a separate thermostat to confirm that the one on the smoker is accurate.

Long Meat Tongs

Your old pair of pasta tongs aren't going to cut it when it comes to smoking. You want a sturdy, long pair that lets you grip and turn meat around in the smoker. Pay attention to the actual "claw" part, too, because you don't want the tongs to accidentally tear about the meat when you're turning a piece. For shredding meat, bear claw tongs are very useful.

A Smoker Cover

To protect your smoker against the elements, you need a cover to keep it clean and dry. Waterproof covers made from polyester material are very popular.

III. Cleaning Your Electric Smoker

Once you've used your smoker and eaten your fill of delicious food, it's time for cleanup. This part is never fun, but it's essential for your smoker. Keeping it clean ensures it has a long life and keeps producing great food. You should always clean your smoker after each use and then every once and a while, give it a really big clean. Keep an eye out for mold, rust, and scale.

The After-Each-BBQ Clean:

1. Unplug the smoker and wait until it's completely cool.

2. Take out everything that you can remove - the racks, smoker box, water pan, and drip tray.

3. With a grill brush, scrape off the black, carbonized bits of food off the racks. Don't scrub too hard or you'll rub off the protective seasoning. You should also never use an abrasive cleaner, like an oven cleaner. A natural cleaner from Traeger should work.

4. Open the smoker box and toss out the ash. Wipe down the box with hot soapy water, rinse, and dry.

5. Clean the drip tray with degreasing soap and water. Rinse and dry. Repeat with the water pan.

6. For the wood chip drawer, wipe it down with a clean cloth and degreaser. Fill a spray bottle with water to rinse if the drawer isn't removable. If it is, you can just rinse it out under a sink. Dry well before returning to the smoker.

7. For the rest of the smoker, you can use a mixture of apple cider vinegar and hot water. You don't need to rinse off this solution. A spray bottle is a convenient tool. Wipe down the areas you've sprayed with a clean cloth to remove all the smoke residue. Note: Avoid any actual electrical parts.

8. If you see ash hanging around anywhere in your smoker, vacuum it up. Ash attracts moisture, which in turn attracts mold and causes rusting.

9. Put the removable parts back into your smoker. It's ready to be used again!

PORK & BEEF RECIPES

01. CRAZY SMOKED PORK SPARE RIBS

Preparation Time: 5 hours
Cooking Time: 4 hours
Serving: 6
Preferred Wood Chip: Hickory

Ingredients:

- 6 pound of pork spareribs

For Dry Rub

- ½ a cup of packed brown sugar
- 2 tablespoon of chili powder
- 1 tablespoon of paprika
- 1 tablespoon of freshly ground black pepper
- 2 tablespoon of garlic powder
- 2 teaspoon of onion powder
- 2 teaspoon of kosher salt
- 2 teaspoon of ground cumin
- 1 teaspoon of ground cinnamon
- 1 teaspoon of jalapeno seasoning salt
- 1 teaspoon of Cayenne pepper

For Mop Sauce

- 1 cup of apple cider
- ¾ cup of apple cider vinegar
- 1 tablespoon of onion powder
- 1 tablespoon of garlic powder
- 2 tablespoon of lemon juice
- 1 jalapeno pepper finely chopped up
- 3 tablespoon of hot pepper sauce
- Kosher salt as needed
- Black pepper as needed
- 2 cups of soaked wood chips

Directions:

1. Take a medium sized bowl and add brown sugar, chili powder, 2 tablespoon of garlic powder, 2 teaspoon of onion powder, cumin, cinnamon, kosher salt, cayenne pepper, jalapeno seasoning
2. Mix well and rub the mixture over the pork spare ribs
3. Allow it to refrigerate for 4 hours
4. Heat up your smoker to 250-degree Fahrenheit
5. Take a medium bowl and stir in apple cider, apple cider vinegar, 1 tablespoon of onion powder, jalapeno, 1 tablespoon of garlic powder, salt, pepper and lemon juice
6. Add a handful of soaked wood chips and transfer the ribs to your smoker middle rack
7. Smoke for 3-4 hours making sure to keep adding chips after every hour
8. Take the meat out and serve!

Nutrition Value:

Calories: 1591
Fats: 120g
Carbs: 44g
Fiber: 3g

02. SMOKED "ONION SOUP" PORK

Preparation Time: 2 hours
Cooking Time: 4 hours 30 minutes
Serving: 6
Preferred Wood Chip: Pecan

Ingredients:

- A rack of pork spare ribs
- 2 packs of onion soup mix
- Barbecue pork rib rub (with salt, garlic powder, pepper and paprika)
- 4 cups of water

Directions:

1. Remove the white membrane off the pork meat and trim off

any excess fat
2. Pre-heat your smoker to 250 degree Fahrenheit
3. Prepare your rub mixture by mixing salt, garlic powder, pepper and paprika in a bowl
4. Rub the rib with the mixture
5. Transfer to the smoker and smoker for 2 hours
6. Blend 2 packs of onion soup with 4 cups of water
7. Once smoking is complete, take a heavy aluminum foil and transfer the meat to the foil, pour the soup mix all over
8. Seal the ribs
9. Smoke for another 1 and a ½ hours
10. Gently open the foil and turn the rib, seal it up and smoke for 1 hour more
11. Slice and serve!

Nutrition Value:
Calories: 461
Fats: 22g
Carbs: 17g
Fiber: 4g

03. DAMN FEISTY PORK BUTT

Preparation Time: 2 hours + 4 hours soak time
Cooking Time: 20 minutes
Serving: 18 hours
Preferred Wood Chip: Pecan

Ingredients:

- 7 pound of fresh pork butt roast
- 2 tablespoon of ground New Mexico Chile Powder
- 4 tablespoon of packed up brown sugar

Directions:

1. Start off by soaking up your Pork Butt in a finely prepared brine (salt) solution for 4 hours at least and overnight at max
2. Make sure to cover the Butt up before placing it in your fridge
3. Pre-heat your smoker to a temperature of 200-225 degree

Fahrenheit

4. Take a small sized bowl and toss in the chili powder, brown sugar alongside any other seasoning which you may fancy
5. Rub the butt with your prepared mixture finely
6. Finely take a roasting rack and place it in a drip pan
7. Lay your butt on top of the rack
8. Smoke the butt about 6-18 hours (Keep in mind that the pork will be done once the temperature of its internals reaches 100 degree Fahrenheit)
9. Serve hot

Nutrition Value:

Calories: 326
Fats: 21g
Carbs:4g
Fiber: 0.5g

04. DELICIOUS MAPLE GLAZED SMOKED BACON

Preparation Time: 7 days
Cooking Time: 15 hours
Serving: 6
Preferred Wood Chip: Maple/Apple/Cherry Woods

Ingredients:

- 1 and a ½ gallons of water
- 2 tablespoon of sodium nitrate
- 1 cup of sugar based curing mix
- 2 cups of coarse salt
- 1 cup of brown sugar
- 1 , 14 pound whole pork belly

Directions:

1. Take a large sized kettle and add water, sodium nitrate, brown sugar, curing salt and maple syrup
2. Mix well and bring the whole mixture to a boil over high-heat
3. Cook for 15 minutes until everything is dissolved

4. Pour the mixture into a 5 gallon plastic bucket and allow it to cool down to room temperature
5. Cut the pork belly against the grain into 4-6 slabs and transfer to your bring bucket, place a weight on top if needed to fully submerge them
6. Cover and allow them to refrigerate for 7 days
7. When ready to smoke, remove the pork from the brine mix and rinse under cold water
8. Allow the pieces to stand under open air/fan for 1-2 hours until dry
9. Smoke the slabs at 110 degree Fahrenheit for 8-12 hours, making sure to keep adding more chips after every 1 hour
10. Remove, slice and serve!

Nutrition Value:
Calories: 191
Fats: 11g
Carbs: 12g
Fiber: 1g

05. THE SPACIOUS HOME MADE BACON

Preparation Time: 20 minutes + 10 days curing time
Cooking Time: 4 hours
Serving: 10
Preferred Wood Chip: Apple/Hickory

Ingredients:
- 2 tablespoon of pink curing salt
- 2 tablespoon of sugar
- 1 tablespoon of freshly ground black pepper
- 1 pork belly with skin removed and cut up into 3-4 pieces

Directions:
1. Take a small bowl and add curing salt, sugar and pepper
2. Rub the whole pork pieces with the spice mix and transfer the pieces to a re-sealable bag
3. Cover tightly and refrigerate for 8-10 days, allowing it to cure
4. Once ready, pre-heat your smoker to 200 degree Fahrenheit

using your desired wood
5. Rinse the pork belly pieces well under cold water and pat them try
6. Transfer to your smoker rack and smoke for 4 hours until the internal temperature reaches 150 degree Fahrenheit
7. Allow the meat to cool for 30-40 minutes
8. Refrigerate for a few hours and slice
9. Enjoy!

Nutrition Value:

Calories: 279
Fats: 12g
Carbs: 32g
Fiber: 2g

06. CURIOUSLY SMOKED ITALIAN SAUSAGES

Preparation Time: 5 minutes
Cooking Time: 3-4 hours
Serving: 6
Preferred Wood Chip: Apple/Hickory

Ingredients:
- 2 pound of Italian sausage
- 8-12 hot dog buns
- Your desired condiment such as Mustard or Ketchup

Directions:
1. Pre-heat your smoker to 250 degree Fahrenheit using your desired wood chip
2. Transfer fresh sausage to your smoker rack and smoke for 3-4 hours until the internal temperature reaches 165 degree Fahrenheit
3. Wrap the buns tightly in aluminum foil and transfer to smoker
4. Smoke for 10-15 minutes more
5. Serve sausages with the buns with your desired toppings
6. Enjoy!

Nutrition Value:

Calories: 234
Fats: 18g
Carbs: 2g
Fiber: 2g

07. ULTIMATE CHUCK ROAST

Preparation Time: 15 minutes
Cooking Time: 4-5 hours
Serving: 6
Preferred Wood Chip: Apple/Hickory

Ingredients:

- 1 whole 4-5 pound chuck roast
- ¼ cup of olive oil
- ¼ cup of firmly packed brown sugar
- 2 tablespoon of Cajun seasoning
- 2 tablespoon of paprika
- 2 tablespoon of cayenne pepper

Directions:

1. Pre-heat your smoker to 225 degree Fahrenheit using oak wood
2. Rub chuck roast all over with olive oil
3. Take a small bowl and add brown sugar, paprika, Cajun seasoning, cayenne
4. Coat the roast well with spice mix
5. Transfer the transfer the chuck roast to smoker rack and smoke for 4-5 hours
6. Once the internal temperature reaches 165 degree Fahrenheit, take the meat out and slice
7. Enjoy!

Nutrition Value:

Calories: 219
Fats: 16g
Carbs: 0g
Fiber: 3g

08. JUICY GLAZE HAM

Preparation Time: 15 minutes
Cooking Time: 2 hours
Serving: 10
Preferred Wood Chip: Apple/Hickory

Ingredients:

- 10 pound of bone-in spiral cut ham
- ½ a cup of canned pineapple juice
- ¼ cup of light brown sugar
- 1 tablespoon of Worcestershire sauce
- ½ a teaspoon of coarse kosher salt
- ¼ teaspoon of ground cloves
- ¼ teaspoon of ground nutmeg
- 1 teaspoon of cornstarch
- ¼ cup of water

Directions:

1. Pre-heat your smoker at this point to a temperature of 250 degree Fahrenheit
2. Place your Ham directly on the smoker rack
3. Once the ham starts to smoke, take a small saucepan and add the pine apple juice, brown sugar, salt, Worcestershire, nutmeg to make the glaze
4. Heat it on top of your stove over medium heat while making sure to stir it as the sugar dissolves
5. Take another bowl and combine some cornstarch with water and mix well
6. Slowly pour the liquid into the boiling glaze whisking up the lumps away
7. Let the mixture boil for a minute and remove the glaze
8. Reserve half of the mix for glaze
9. Baste the ham with the glaze and toss in the wood chips after every 30 minutes for the next 2 hours
10. Once the internal temperature reaches 140 degree Fahrenheit, it is done
11. Let it cool and glaze it with some more mix if you desire
12. Serve hot

Nutrition Value:

Calories: 157

Fats: 6g

Carbs: 5g

Fiber: 1g

09. SMOKED STEAK STRIPS

Servings: 6

Preparation Time: 15 minutes

Ingredients:

- 2 tsp. freshly ground black pepper
- 1 tbsp. garlic powder
- 1/2 tbsp. salt
- 1/4 tbsp. dry mustard
- 2 (12-ounce) New York strip or sirloin strip steaks, trimmed
- 2 tsp. Worcestershire sauce
- Smoke Time: 1 Hour, 15 Mins
- Smoke Temp: 225

Directions:

1. Combine the mustard, pepper, salt, and garlic powder all in one small bowl. Rub this on both sides of the steak strips. Place these coated pieces in a plastic bag. Toss in the Worcestershire sauce. Seal to coat the sauce all over the steak strips, and seal. Allow them to marinate in the fridge for half an hour.
2. Arrange the steaks on the rack of the smoker. In a spare pan pour two cups of water into it, and place it in the smoker over a place that doesn't have direct heat.
3. Close the lid of the smoker and allow steaks to smoke.
4. Once the steaks are done serve over rice or with some steamed vegetables.

10. SLOW SMOKED PORTERHOUSE STEAKS

Servings: 4

Preparation Time: 15 minutes

Ingredients:

- 2 whole porterhouse steaks, at least 1 1/2 inches thick (30 to 40 ounces each)
- Kosher salt
- freshly ground black pepper
- Smoke Time: 2 Hours
- Smoke Temp: 200

Directions:

1. On each steak, season them on both sides with salt and pepper.
2. Place the steaks on a cutting board, and insert metal skewers, at least 3 or 4 so the steaks are secure. Afterwards turn the steaks to the side so the skewers are holding them upright.
3. Place steaks in the smoker. The internal temperatures of the steaks should be 120 degrees, and then they're ready to eat.

11. SMOKED ULTIMATE FLANK STEAK

Servings: 3
Preparation Time: 20 minutes

Ingredients:

- 1 1/2-2 lbs flank steaks
- 1/4 cup madeira wine
- 1/4 cup olive oil
- 1 tbsp. lemon pepper
- 1/2 tbsp. black pepper
- 1 tbsp. sea salt or 1 tbsp. kosher salt
- 1/8 cup soy sauce or 1/8 cup Worcestershire sauce
- 3 garlic cloves, crushed
- 1/2 tbsp. marjoram
- Smoke Time: 1 ½ Hours
- Smoke Temp: 250

Directions:

1. Put the steak in a bag. Add in the rest of the ingredients, and shake around to coat the steak evenly.
2. Allow the steak to marinate for 6 to 12 hours. During the time it's marinating, be sure to turn the steak over at least four times.
3. Smoke the steak. Once done serve with preferred sides.

12. SWEET COLA RIBS

Servings: 4
Preparation Time: 15 minutes

Ingredients:
Sweet Cola Barbecue Sauce:
- 1 tbsp. vegetable oil
- 1 medium onion, finely chopped
- 3 cloves garlic, finely chopped
- 2 cups ketchup
- 1 can cola
- 1/2 cup apple cider vinegar
- 2 tsp. brown sugar
- 1/2 tbsp. fresh ground black pepper
- 1/2 tbsp. onion powder
- 1/2 tbsp. ground mustard
- 1/2 tbsp. lemon juice
- 1 tbsp. Worcestershire sauce

Dry Rub:
- 2 tsp. salt
- 2 tsp. brown sugar
- 2 tsp. garlic powder
- 2 tsp. onion powder
- 1 tbsp. ground cumin
- 1 tbsp. chili powder
- 1 tbsp. black pepper
- 2 racks pork spare ribs (about 3 lb. each)
- Smoke Time: 1 Hour, 15 Mins

- Smoke Temp: 25

Directions:

1. Head up a medium saucepan over medium heat. Add in the oil. Once it's heated up, add onion and garlic. Sauté them until they become tender. Add the rest of the sauce ingredients, and bring it all to a boil. Reduce the heat, and then allow it to simmer for one hour and fifteen minutes.
2. In a small bowl, combine all the dry rub ingredients.
3. Rinse the ribs off. Be sure to dry them. Pull off any excess membrane or fat from the ribs. Season both sides as much as you please with the dry rub and sauce. Be sure to store the ribs in the fridge for four to twelve hours.
4. Place the ribs in the smoker. Flip them a couple of times while they're smoking.
5. Serve ribs while still warm.

13. EASY-PEASY SMOKED RIBS

Servings: 2
Preparation Time: 15 minutes

Ingredients:

- 1 - 2 racks baby back pork ribs
- 1 - 8 oz bottle Kraft honey hickory smoke barbecue sauce
- Sweet & Smokey BBQ Rub
- Steak Seasoning
- 1/2 - cup brown sugar
- Olive Oil
- Smoke Time: 1 Hour
- Smoke Temp: 225

Directions:

1. Cut the membrane off the ribs.
2. Rub the olive oil over the ribs on both sides. Apply the dry rub to the ribs and the steak seasoning.
3. Place the ribs in the fridge after wrapping them up in plastic wrap. Store them in the fridge for six hours or overnight.
4. Allow the rips to sit out for half an hour prior to smoking

them.

5. Place a piece of foil on the rack. Place the ribs in the smoker, and allow them to smoke for two and a half hours.
6. Slather the ribs with barbecue sauce. Add some brown sugar to the barbecue sauce to make the ribs sweeter. Wrap them up in foil afterward.
7. Allow the ribs to cool for a few minutes before eating.

14. MEMPHIS STYLE BEEF RIBS

Servings: 4
Preparation Time: 15 minutes

Ingredients:
BBQ Dry Rub:
- 1 1/2 cups paprika
- 3/4 cup sugar
- 3 3/4 tsp. onion powder
- 4 (about 4 lb.s each) slabs beef spare ribs
- Smoke Time: 2 Hours, 45 Mins
- Smoke Temp: 250

Directions:
1. In a small bowl mix together all the dry rub ingredients. This rub can be used on multiple ribs or store for later.
2. Rinse the ribs off and dry them. Apply the dry rub to the ribs. Wrap them up in plastic wrap and store in the fridge for eight hours.
3. Place ribs in the smoker.
4. After the first two hours turn the ribs over. Allow them to smoke for the rest of the allotted time.
5. Serve while still warm.

15. SMOKED BURGERS

Servings: 4
Preparation Time: 10 minutes

Ingredients:

- 4 Hamburger Patties (hand shaped, using your preferred ground beef)
- 4 slices Provolone Cheese
- Season All
- Large Onion (with a beef bullion cube and a pat of butter)
- Vlasic Farmers Garden Pickle Chips
- Smoke Time: 30 Mins
- Smoke Temp: 250

Directions:
1. Sprinkle the season all on each side of the burger patties.
2. Cut the onion into slices. In a foil square, place the onion in the middle. Do the same for a bouillon cube and some butter. Seal up the foil.
3. Put the patties and onion inside the smoker.
4. Serve the burgers up with the cooked onion on top, pickle chips, mustard, and provolone cheese.

16. HICKORY SMOKED BURGERS

Servings: 12
Preparation Time: 15 minutes

Ingredients:
- 2 lb.s lean ground round (can use ground turkey for a low-fat burger)
- 1 package dry onion soup mix
- 1/2 cup water
- 1 tbsp. hot sauce
- 3/4 cup bread crumbs (if desired)
- Worcestershire sauce
- Smoke Time: 20 Mins
- Smoke Temp: 250

Directions:
1. Place all the ingredients in a large bowl and mix together.
2. Roll the beef into patties it should yield 12 to 14 of them.
3. Place the patties in the smoker. Flip over halfway through

smoking.

4. When they're ready serve immediately.

17. SMOKED BEEF BRISKET

Servings: 6
Preparation Time: 10 minutes

Ingredients:

- 1 1/2 cups paprika
- 3/4 cup sugar
- 3 tsp. onion powder
- 3 tsp. garlic salt
- 1 tsp. celery salt
- 1 tsp. black pepper
- 1 tbsp. lemon pepper
- 1 tbsp. mustard powder
- 1 tbsp. cayenne
- 1/2 tbsp. dried thyme
- 1 trimmed brisket, about 5 to 6 lb.s
- Smoke Time: 7 Hours
- Smoke Temp: 250

Directions:

1. In a small bowl mix together all dry ingredients. Be sure they are blended very well.
2. Trim ¼ inch of fat from the brisket. Be sure to season the brisket with only ¼ cup of the rub you made earlier.
3. Smoke the brisket over indirect heat. Flip it over halfway into smoking.
4. Once the brisket is done, allow it to cool for ten minutes before serving.

18. BASIC BRISKET

Servings: 12
Preparation time: 45 minutes
Cooking time: 8 to 9 hours plus 1 to 2 hours resting

Ingredients:

- 1 full "whole packer" beef brisket (12 to 15 pounds)
- 1/2 cup brown sugar (divided)
- 1/4 cup chili powder
- 1/4 cup sweet paprika
- 1/4 cup kosher salt, plus more to taste
- 2 tablespoons garlic powder
- 2 tablespoons onion powder
- 2 tablespoons ground cumin
- 1 tablespoon ancho chili powder
- 1 tablespoon freshly ground black pepper, plus more to taste
- 1 teaspoon cayenne pepper, plus more to taste
- 4 tablespoons butter (melted)

Directions:

1. Pour 2 cups water into the Masterbuilt smoker's water pan. Place a mixture of hickory and apple wood chips in the smoker's wood tray and preheat smoker to 250°F.
2. Thoroughly rinse brisket with cold water and pat dry with paper towels. Trim brisket as necessary to about 1/4" fat and trim fat between the flat and the deckle (separate portions if necessary to fit in smoker).
3. Mix 1/4 cup brown sugar with chili powder, paprika, salt, garlic powder, onion powder, cumin, ancho chili powder, black pepper and cayenne pepper and rub all over brisket.
4. Place brisket fat-side down on smoker grate and smoke until the internal temperature of the meat reaches 165°F, about 6 hours. Add wood chips to the wood tray as necessary.
5. Mix butter and remaining 1/4 cup brown sugar and brush all over brisket. Wrap brisket in two layers of aluminum foil and continue smoking until the internal temperature of the meat reaches 200°F, 2 to 3 hours more.
6. Remove brisket from smoker and let rest for 1 to 2 hours. Slice brisket against the grain and serve with barbecue sauce as desired. Enjoy!

Nutrition Values:

Calories: 358; Total Fat: 23g; Saturated Fat: 11g; Protein: 29g; Carbs: 9g; Fiber: 2g; Sugar: 4g

19. CENTRAL TEXAS-STYLE BRISKET

Servings: 12
Preparation time: 45 minutes
Cooking time: 8 to 9 hours plus 1 to 2 hours resting

Ingredients:

- 1 full "whole packer" beef brisket (12 to 15 pounds)
- 1/2 cup kosher salt, plus more to taste
- 1/2 cup black pepper, plus more to taste
- 2 teaspoons onion powder
- 1 tablespoon garlic powder

Directions:

1. Pour 2 cups water into the Masterbuilt smoker's water pan. Place mesquite wood chips in the smoker's wood tray and preheat smoker to 250°F.
2. Thoroughly rinse brisket with cold water and pat dry with paper towels. Trim brisket as necessary to about 1/4" fat and trim fat between the flat and the deckle (separate portions if necessary to fit in smoker).
3. Mix salt, pepper, onion powder and garlic powder and rub all over brisket.
4. Place brisket fat-side down on smoker grate and smoke until the internal temperature of the meat reaches 165°F, about 6 hours. Add wood chips to the wood tray as necessary.
5. Wrap brisket in two layers of aluminum foil and continue smoking until the internal temperature of the meat reaches 200°F, 2 to 3 hours more. Add wood chips to the wood tray as necessary.
6. Remove brisket from smoker and let rest for 1 to 2 hours. Slice brisket against the grain and serve. Enjoy!

Nutrition Values:

Calories: 315; Total Fat: 20g; Saturated Fat: 8g; Protein: 29g; Carbs: 5g; Fiber: 2g; Sugar: 0g

20. KANSAS CITY BRISKET SANDWICHES

Servings: 16
Preparation time: 1 hour
Cooking time: 8 to 9 hours

Ingredients:
- 1 full "whole packer" beef brisket (12 to 15 pounds)
- 3 tablespoons kosher salt, plus more to taste
- 2 tablespoons freshly ground black pepper, plus more to taste
- 2 tablespoons garlic powder
- 2 tablespoons onion powder
- 1 tablespoon ground mustard
- 1 teaspoon cayenne pepper, plus more to taste
- 1 package (12 to 14 ounces) frozen beer battered onion rings
- 16 Kaiser rolls
- 4 tablespoons butter (softened)
- 16 deli slices provolone cheese
- 1 bottle (18 ounces) KC Masterpiece barbecue sauce

Directions:
1. Pour 2 cups water into the Masterbuilt smoker's water pan. Place hickory or cherry wood chips in the smoker's wood tray and preheat smoker to 250°F.
2. Thoroughly rinse brisket with cold water and pat dry with paper towels. Trim brisket as necessary to about 1/4" fat and trim fat between the flat and the deckle (separate portions if necessary to fit in smoker).
3. Mix salt, pepper, garlic powder, onion powder, ground mustard and cayenne pepper and rub all over brisket.
4. Place brisket fat-side down on smoker grate and smoke until the internal temperature of the meat reaches 180°F, about 7

hours. Add wood chips to the wood tray as necessary.

5. Cover brisket with aluminum foil and continue smoking until the internal temperature of the meat reaches 200°F, 1 to 2 hours more. Add wood chips to the wood tray as necessary.
6. Remove brisket from smoker, cover with aluminum foil and let rest while you prepare the frozen onion rings according to package directions, about 30 minutes.
7. Spread butter over cut surfaces of rolls and toast in preheated oven until golden, 7 to 8 minutes.
8. Thinly slice brisket against the grain and pile onto roll heels. Top meat with cheese slices, barbecue sauce and onion rings and serve immediately. Enjoy!

Nutrition Values:

Calories: 665; Total Fat: 35g; Saturated Fat: 17g; Protein: 35g; Carbs: 53g; Fiber: 3g; Sugar: 13g

21. KANSAS CITY BURNT ENDS

Servings: 6
Preparation time: 1 hour
Cooking time: 6 to 7 hours

Ingredients:

- 1 brisket point (4 to 5 pounds)
- 1/2 cup brown sugar
- 1/2 cup white sugar
- 1/4 cup kosher salt, plus more to taste
- 1/4 cup chili powder
- 1/4 cup coarsely ground black pepper, plus more to taste
- 3 tablespoons paprika
- 3 tablespoons ground cumin
- 2 teaspoons cayenne pepper, plus more to taste
- 1 tablespoon garlic powder
- 1 tablespoon onion powder
- 1 tablespoon butter
- 1/4 cup minced onion

- 4 garlic cloves (minced)
- 1 cup ketchup
- 1 cup tomato sauce
- 3/4 cup red wine vinegar
- 1/4 cup molasses
- 1 teaspoon hickory-flavored liquid smoke, plus more to taste
- Dash cinnamon or ginger

Directions:

1. Pour 2 cups water into the Masterbuilt smoker's water pan. Place hickory or cherry wood chips in the smoker's wood tray and preheat smoker to 225°F.
2. Thoroughly rinse brisket point with cold water, pat dry with paper towels and trim fat to 1/4". Mix brown sugar, white sugar, salt, chili powder, black pepper, paprika, cumin and cayenne pepper. Set aside about 1/3 of the spice mixture to make the sauce. Add garlic powder and onion powder to remaining spice mixture and rub over brisket.
3. Place brisket fat-side down on smoker grate and smoke until the internal temperature of the meat reaches 175°F, about 5 hours. Add wood chips to the wood tray as necessary.
4. Wrap brisket in aluminum foil and continue smoking until the internal temperature of the meat reaches 200°F, 1 to 2 hours more. Add wood chips to the wood tray as necessary.
5. Meanwhile, for the sauce, melt butter in a medium saucepan over medium-low heat and sauté onion until tender, about 5 minutes, stirring frequently. Add garlic and sauté about 1 minute more, stirring constantly. Add ketchup, tomato sauce, vinegar, molasses, liquid smoke and reserved spice mixture and season to taste with salt and pepper. Heat sauce to a boil, stirring occasionally. Reduce heat and simmer to thicken to desired consistency, stirring occasionally, 10 to 15 minutes.
6. Remove wrapped brisket from smoker and let rest for about 30 minutes. Remove foil from brisket, saving the cooking juices. Chop brisket into 1" chunks and toss with the cooking juices. Serve burnt ends with the sauce and enjoy!

Nutrition Values:

Calories: 432; Total Fat: 22g; Saturated Fat: 9g; Protein: 30g; Carbs:

29g; Fiber: 3g; Sugar: 19g

22. PRIME RIB

Servings: 8
Preparation time: 30 minutes
Cooking time: 5 1/2 hours

Ingredients:
- 1 prime rib roast (about 8 pounds)
- 2 tablespoons horseradish mustard
- 2 tablespoons peppercorns
- 1 tablespoon kosher salt
- 2 teaspoons dried rosemary
- 2 teaspoons dried thyme
- 1 teaspoon white sugar
- 1/2 teaspoon red pepper flakes

Directions:
1. Pour about 2 cups water into the Masterbuilt smoker's water pan. Place hickory wood chips in the smoker's wood tray and preheat smoker to 225°F.
2. Trim roast with a sharp knife as necessary to about 1/4" fat. Tie roast in a roll shape with kitchen twine. Rub roast all over with mustard. Pulse peppercorns, salt, rosemary, thyme, sugar and red pepper flakes in a food processor or spice grinder and rub all over roast. (If desired, refrigerate roast, uncovered, for up to 8 hours).
3. Place roast fat-side up on smoker grate and smoke until the internal temperature of the meat reaches 135°F, about 5 1/2 hours for a medium-rare roast (reduce smoking time for a rare roast). Add wood chips to the wood tray as necessary.
4. Remove roast from smoker, cover loosely with aluminum foil and let rest for about 30 minutes. Slice roast as desired and serve. Enjoy!

Nutrition Values:
Calories: 249; Total Fat: 11g; Saturated Fat: 4g; Protein: 47g; Carbs:

0g; Fiber: 0g; Sugar: 0g

23. SANTA MARIA SIRLOIN TIP ROAST

Servings: 6
Preparation time: 30 minutes
Cooking time: 2 1/2 hours

Ingredients:
- 1 sirloin tip roast (about 3 pounds)
- 1/4 cup olive oil (divided)
- 2 tablespoons kosher salt, plus more to taste
- 1 teaspoon coarsely ground black pepper, plus more to taste
- 1 teaspoon garlic powder

Directions:
1. Pour about 2 cups water into the Masterbuilt smoker's water pan. Place red oak or oak wood chips in the smoker's wood tray and preheat smoker to 250°F.
2. Brush roast all over with 2 tablespoons olive oil. Mix salt, pepper and garlic powder and rub all over roast. Heat remaining 2 tablespoons olive oil in a large nonstick skillet and sear until browned on all sides, turning as necessary, about 8 minutes.
3. Place roast on smoker grate and smoke until the internal temperature of the meat reaches 145°F, about 2 1/2 hours for a medium-rare roast (reduce smoking time for a rare roast). Add wood chips to the wood tray as necessary.
4. Remove roast from smoker, cover loosely with aluminum foil and let rest for about 10 minutes. Slice roast as desired and serve. Enjoy!

Nutrition Values:
Calories: 260; Total Fat: 10g; Saturated Fat: 4g; Protein: 41g; Carbs: 0g; Fiber: 0g; Sugar: 0g

24. SANTA CLARA TRI-TIP ROAST

Servings: 6
Preparation time: 15 minutes
Cooking time: 1 1/2 hours

Ingredients:

- 1 tri-tip roast (about 2 1/2 pounds)
- 2 tablespoons olive oil
- 2 teaspoons kosher salt, plus more to taste
- 2 teaspoons freshly ground black pepper
- 1 teaspoon garlic salt
- 1 teaspoon dried parsley

Directions:

1. Pour about 2 cups water into the Masterbuilt smoker's water pan. Place red oak or oak wood chips in the smoker's wood tray and preheat smoker to 250°F.
2. Remove silver skin from roast if necessary and brush roast with olive oil. Mix salt, pepper and garlic powder and rub all over roast.
3. Place roast on smoker grate and smoke until the internal temperature of the meat reaches 130°F, about 1 1/2 hours.
4. Remove roast from smoker, wrap tightly with aluminum foil and let rest for about 20 minutes. Cut roast against the grain into 1/4" thick slices and serve. Enjoy!

Nutrition Values:

Calories: 471; Total Fat: 24g; Saturated Fat: 8g; Protein: 63g; Carbs: 00g; Fiber: 0g; Sugar: 0g

25. BEEF SHORT RIBS

Servings: 6
Preparation time: 45 minutes
Cooking time: 5 to 6 hours

Ingredients:

- 12 beef short ribs (about 6 pounds, about 5" long)

- 1 cup yellow mustard
- 2 tablespoons soy sauce
- 2 tablespoons apple cider vinegar
- 1 tablespoon lime juice
- 2 tablespoons kosher salt, plus more to taste
- 2 tablespoons freshly ground black pepper, plus more to taste
- 2 tablespoons brown sugar
- 2 tablespoons garlic powder
- 1 tablespoon sweet paprika

Directions:

1. Pour about 2 cups water into the Masterbuilt smoker's water pan. Place pecan or cherry wood chips in the smoker's wood tray and preheat smoker to 225°F.
2. Remove silver skin from ribs if necessary, trim fat if desired and score ribs along the bones with a sharp knife. Mix mustard, soy sauce, vinegar and lime juice and rub all over ribs. Mix salt, pepper, brown sugar, garlic powder and paprika and rub all over ribs. Let ribs stand for about 15 minutes.
3. Place ribs bone-sides down on smoker grate and smoke until tender and the internal temperature of the meat reaches 190°F, 5 to 6 hours. Add wood chips to the wood tray as necessary.
4. Remove ribs from smoker, cover loosely with aluminum foil and let rest for about 15 minutes. Cut ribs into individual pieces and serve with barbecue sauce if desired. Enjoy!

Nutrition Values:

Calories: 284; Total Fat: 16 g; Saturated Fat: 7g; Protein: 31g; Carbs: 5g; Fiber: 1g Sugar: 3g

26. SHORT RIBS TEXAS-STYLE

Servings: 6
Preparation time: 45 minutes plus 12 to 24 hours refrigeration

Cooking time: 6 to 7 hours

Ingredients:

- 12 beef short ribs (about 6 pounds, about 5" long)
- 1/3 cup kosher salt (divided)
- 3 tablespoons coarsely ground black pepper
- 2 tablespoons paprika
- 2 tablespoon chili powder
- 1 tablespoon cayenne pepper, plus more to taste
- 1 tablespoon garlic powder
- 1 tablespoon onion powder
- 1 cup beef broth
- 1/2 cup butter (melted)

Directions:

1. Remove silver skin from ribs if necessary and trim fat. Using a sharp knife, cut ribs into portions with 2 bones each. Rub ribs all over with about 1 tablespoon salt, place in a covered container and refrigerate for 12 to 24 hours.
2. Pour about 2 cups water into the Masterbuilt smoker's water pan. Place oak or hickory wood chips in the smoker's wood tray and preheat smoker to 225°F.
3. Mix remaining salt with pepper, paprika, chili powder, cayenne pepper, garlic powder and onion powder. Set aside about 2 tablespoons spice mixture. Rub remaining spice mixture all over ribs. Let ribs stand for about 15 minutes.
4. Place ribs bone-sides down on smoker grate and smoke for about 1 hour.
5. Mix reserved spice mixture, broth and butter and mop over ribs. Continue smoking until ribs are tender and the internal temperature of the meat reaches 200°F, 4 to 5 more hours mopping about every hour (briefly microwave mop sauce as needed to re-melt the butter). Add wood chips to the wood tray as necessary.
6. Remove ribs from smoker, cover loosely with aluminum foil and let rest for about 15 minutes. Cut ribs into individual pieces and serve with barbecue sauce if desired. Enjoy!

Nutrition Values:

Calories: 385; Total Fat: 30g; Saturated Fat: 15g; Protein: 30g; Carbs: 0g; Fiber: 0g Sugar: 0g

POULTRY

27. AUTHENTIC CITRUS SMOKED CHICKEN

Preparation Time: 15 minutes
Cooking Time: 18 hours 5 minutes
Serving: 12
Preferred Wood Chip: Pecan/Maple/Peach

Ingredients:

- 1 whole chicken
- 4 cups of lemon-lime flavored carbonated beverage
- 1 tablespoon of garlic powder
- 2 cups of soaked wood chips

Directions:

1. Transfer the whole chicken to a large sized zip bag
2. Sprinkle garlic powder and pour lemon-lime soda mix into the bag
3. Seal the bag and allow it to marinate overnight
4. Pre-heat your electric smoker to 225 degree Fahrenheit
5. Remove the chicken from the bag and transfer to your smoker rack
6. Discard the marinade
7. Smoker for 10 hours, making sure keep adding more wood chips after every hour
8. Serve and enjoy!

Nutrition Value:

Calories: 644
Fats: 34g
Carbs: 19g
Fiber: 0.1g

28. AMAZING MESQUITE MAPLE AND BACON CHICKEN

Preparation Time: 20 minutes
Cooking Time: 1 and a ½ to 2 hours
Serving: 7
Preferred Wood Chip: Mesquite

Ingredients:

- 4 boneless and skinless chicken breast
- Salt as needed
- Freshly ground black pepper
- 12 slices of uncooked bacon
- 1 cup of maple syrup
- ½ a cup of melted butter
- 1 teaspoon of liquid smoke

Directions:

1. Pre-heat your smoker to 250 degree Fahrenheit
2. Season the chicken with pepper and salt
3. Wrap the breast with 3 bacon slices and cover the entire surface
4. Secure the bacon with tooth picks
5. Take a medium sized bowl and stir in maple syrup, butter, liquid smoker and mix well
6. Reserve 1/3rd of this mixture for later use
7. Submerge the chicken breast into the butter mix and coat them well
8. Place a pan in your smoker and transfer the chicken to your smoker
9. Smoker for 1 to 1 and a ½ hours
10. Brush the chicken with reserved butter and smoke for 30 minutes more until the internal temperature reaches 165 degree Fahrenheit
11. Enjoy!

Nutrition Value:

Calories: 458
Fats: 20g

Carbs: 65g
Fiber: 1g

29. SMOKED PAPRIKA CHICKEN

Preparation Time: 20 minutes
Cooking Time: 2-4 hours
Serving: 4
Preferred Wood Chip: Mesquite

Ingredients:

- 4-6 chicken breast
- 4 tablespoon of olive oil
- 2 tablespoon of smoked paprika
- ½ a tablespoon of kosher salt
- ¼ teaspoon of ground black pepper
- 2 teaspoon of garlic powder
- 2 teaspoon of garlic salt
- 2 teaspoon of black pepper
- 1 teaspoon of cayenne pepper
- 1 teaspoon of rosemary

Directions:

1. Pre-heat your smoker to 220 degree Fahrenheit using your favorite wood chips
2. Prepare your chicken breast according to your desired shapes and transfer to a greased baking dish
3. Take a medium bowl and add spices, stir well
4. Press the spice mix over chicken and transfer the chicken to smoker
5. Smoke for 1-1 and a ½ hours
6. Turn-over and cook for 30 minutes more
7. Once the internal temperature reaches 165 degree Fahrenheit
8. Remove from the smoker and cover with foil
9. Allow it to rest for 15 minutes
10. Enjoy!

Nutrition Value:

Calories: 237

Fats: 6.1g
Carbs: 14g
Fiber: 3g

30. FULLY SMOKED HERBAL QUAIL

Preparation Time: 10 minutes
Cooking Time: 60 minutes
Serving: 8
Preferred Wood Chip: Hickory

Ingredients:

- 4-6 quail
- 2 tablespoon of olive oil
- Salt as needed
- Freshly ground black pepper
- 1 pack of dry Hidden Valley Ranch dressing (or your preferred one)
- ½ a cup of melted butter

Directions:

1. Pre-heat your smoker to 225 degree Fahrenheit using hickory wood
2. Brush the quail with olive oil and season with salt and pepper
3. Place the in your smoker and smoke for 1 hour
4. Take a small bowl and add ranch dressing mix and melted butter
5. After the first 30 minutes of smoking, brush the quail with the ranch mix
6. Repeat again at the end of the cook time
7. Once the internal temperature of the quail reaches 145 degree Fahrenheit, they are ready!

Nutrition Value:

Calories: 209
Fats: 13g
Carbs: 0g
Fiber: 3g

31. HONEY SMOKED TURKEY

Preparation Time: 6 minutes
Cooking Time: 6 hours
Serving: 7
Preferred Wood Chip: Hickory

Ingredients:

- 1 gallon of hot water
- 1 pound of kosher salt
- 2 quarts of vegetable broth
- 8 ounce jars of honey
- 1 cup of orange juice
- 7 pound bag of ice cubes
- 15 pound of whole turkey with giblets and neck removed
- ¼ cup of vegetable oil
- 1 teaspoon of poultry seasoning
- 1 granny smith apples cored and cut up into large chunks
- 1 celery stalk cut up into small chunks
- 1 small sized onion cut up into chunks
- 1 quartered orange

Directions:

1. Take a 54 quart cooler and add kosher salt and hot water
2. Mix them well until everything dissolves
3. Add vegetable broth, orange juice and honey
4. Pour ice cubes into the mix and add the turkey into your brine, keeping the breast side up
5. Lock up the lid of your cooler and let it marinate overnight for 12 hours
6. Make sure that the brine temperature stays under 40 degree Fahrenheit
7. Remove the turkey from the brine and discard the brine
8. Dry the turkey using a kitchen towel
9. Take a bowl and mix vegetable oil and poultry seasoning
10. Rub the turkey with the mixture
11. Place apple, onion, celery and orange pieces inside the cavity of the turkey

12. Pre-heat your smoker to a temperature of 400 degree Fahrenheit and add 1 cup of hickory wood chips
13. Set your turkey onto your smoker and insert a probe into the thickest part of your turkey breast
14. Set the probe for 160 degree Fahrenheit
15. Smoke the turkey for 2 hours until the skin is golden brown
16. Cover the breast, wings and legs using aluminum foil and keep smoking it for 2-3 hours until the probe thermometer reads 160 degree Fahrenheit
17. Make sure to keep adding some hickory chips to your heat box occasionally
18. Remove the vegetables and fruit from the cavity of your Turkey and cover it up with aluminum foil
19. Let it rest of 1 hour and carve it up!

Nutrition Value:
Calories: 353
Fats: 16g
Carbs: 29g
Fiber: 2g

32. ORANGE CRISPY CHICKEN

Preparation Time: 8 hours 30 minutes
Cooking Time: 90 to 120 minutes
Serving: 4
Preferred Wood Chip: Apple

Ingredients:
For Poultry Spice Rub
- 4 teaspoon of paprika
- 1 tablespoon of chili powder
- 2 teaspoon of ground cumin
- 2 teaspoon of dried thyme
- 2 teaspoon of salt
- 2 teaspoon of garlic powder
- 1 teaspoon of freshly ground black pepper
For The Marinade
- 4 chicken quarters

- 2 cups of frozen orange-juice concentrate
- ½ a cup of soy sauce
- 1 tablespoon of garlic powder

Directions:

1. Take a small bowl and add paprika, chili powder, cumin, salt, thyme, garlic powder, pepper and mix well
2. Transfer the chicken quarters to a large dish
3. Take a medium bowl and whisk in orange-juice concentrate, soy sauce, garlic powder, half of the spice-rub mix
4. Pour the marinade over the chicken and cover
5. Refrigerate for 8 hours
6. Pre-heat your smoker to 275 degree Fahrenheit
7. Discard the marinade and rub the surface of the chicken with remaining spice rub
8. Transfer the chicken to smoker and smoker for 1 and a ½ to 2 hours
9. Remove the chicken form the smoker and check using a digital temperature that the internal temperature is 160 degree Fahrenheit
10. Allow it to rest for 10 minutes
11. Enjoy!

Nutrition Value:

Calories: 165
Fats: 8g
Carbs: 14g
Fiber: 2g

33. STANDING SMOKED CHICKEN

Preparation Time: 15 minutes
Cooking Time: 1 and ½ hours – 2 hours
Serving: 6
Preferred Wood Chip: Apple

Ingredients:

- 12 garlic cloves, minced
- 3 whole onions, quartered

- ½ of a quartered lemon
- 1 tablespoon of salt
- 1 teaspoon of black pepper
- 1 and a ½ tablespoon of ground sage
- 1 and a ½ tablespoon of dried thyme
- 1 and a ½ tablespoon of dried rosemary
- 1 teaspoon of paprika
- 1 whole chicken of 4-6 pounds
- 3 tablespoon of vegetable oil

Directions:

1. Remove one or two of the top racks from the smoker to make room for your standing chicken
2. Smash 8 pieces of garlic cloves and add them into the water pan alongside the onion and lemon pieces
3. Pre-heat your smoker to temperature of 250 degree Fahrenheit
4. Finely mince up the rest of the 4 garlic cloves and combine them in a small sized bowl with pepper, salt, sage, rosemary, thyme, paprika and set it aside for later use
5. Remove the giblets from the cavity of the chicken and rinse up the bird finely
6. Pat it dry and rub it up with oil and then with the seasoning mixture created previously
7. Set your chicken in a vertical position on top of your smoker and add in just a handful of soaked chips in the chip loading area
8. Keep adding the chips for every 30 minutes
9. The chicken should be done after about 2 hours when the internal temperature registers 165 degree Fahrenheit
10. Let it cool for 15 minutes and serve

Nutrition Value:

Calories: 128
Fats: 3g
Carbs: 12g
Fiber: 1g

34. EQUALLY WORTHY CINNAMON CURED SMOKED CHICKEN

Preparation Time: 15 minutes + 1 hour brine time
Cooking Time: 1 and a ½ hours
Serving: 4
Preferred Wood Chip: Apple/Cherry

Ingredients:

- 1 quart of water
- ¼ cup of salt
- ¼ cup of firmly packed brown sugar
- 4 chicken breast
- 1 sliced onion
- 1 sliced lemon
- 2 halved cinnamon stick
- 1 tablespoon of ground cinnamon
- 1 tablespoon of red pepper flakes
- 1 tablespoon of seasoned salt

Directions:

1. Take a large bowl and stir in water, brown sugar and salt. Keep stirring until dissolved wel
2. Add chicken, lemon, onion and cinnamon stick to the bowl and cover with plasti wrap
3. Allow it to chill for 1 hour
4. Pre-heat your smoker to 250 degree Fahrenheit with your desired wood
5. Remove the chicken and discard marinade
6. Sprinkle chicken with cinnamon, pepper flakes and seasoning salt
7. Transfer to your smoker rack and smoke for 1 and a ½ hours until the internal temperature reaches 165 degree Fahrenheit
8. Take it out and serve!

Nutrition Value:

Calories: 240
Fats: 5g

Carbs: 2g
Fiber: 1g

35. CITRUS GOOSE BREAST

Preparation Time: 40 minutes
Cooking Time: 6 hours
Serving: 7
Preferred Wood Chip: Hickory

Ingredients:

- ½ a cup of orange juice
- 1/3 cup of olive oil
- 1/3 cup of Dijon mustard
- 1/3 cup of brown sugar
- ¼ cup of soy sauce
- ¼ cup of honey
- 1 tablespoon of dried minced onion
- 1 teaspoon of garlic powder
- 8 goose breast halves

Directions:

1. Take a medium sized bowl and a whisk in orange juice, olive oil, mustard, soy sauce, sugar, honey, onion, garlic powder
2. Mix well and prepare the marinade
3. Transfer the goose breast to the marinade and cover
4. Allow it to refrigerate for 3-6 hours
5. Heat up your smoker to 300 degree Fahrenheit and add some soaked hickory wood chips
6. Transfer the breast to your smoker grate and brush smoke for 6 hours, making sure to keep brushing it with the marinade for the first 30 minutes
7. Keep smoking until the internal temperature reaches 165 degree Fahrenheit
8. Serve and enjoy!

Nutrition Value:

Calories: 1094
Fats: 64g

Carbs: 14g
Fiber: 13g

36. SUPREME CHIPOTLE WINGS

Preparation Time: 75 minutes
Cooking Time: 1 and a ½ to 2 hours
Serving: 8
Preferred Wood Chip: Oak

Ingredients:

- 2 tablespoon packed light brown sugar
- 1 and a ½ tablespoon of chipotle pepper
- 1 tablespoon of Hungarian smoked paprika
- 1 tablespoon of dry mustard
- 1 tablespoon of ground cumin
- 1 and a ½ teaspoon of salt
- 5 and a ½ pound of chicken wings

Directions:

1. Take a small sized bowl and add brown sugar, paprika, chipotle, mustard, salt and cumin
2. Transfer the chicken wings to a large re-sealable bag and pour the seasoning mix
3. Seal and shake the chicken
4. Refrigerate for 60 minutes
5. Pre-heat your smoker to 250 degree Fahrenheit with oak woods
6. Transfer the chicken to your smoker rack and smoke for 1 and a ½ to 2 hours
7. Check if the internal temperature is 165 degree Fahrenheit and serve!

Nutrition Value:

Calories: 180
Fats: 7g
Carbs: 3g
Fiber: 1g

37. TENDER SWEET SRIRACHA BBQ CHICKEN

Preparation Time: 30 minutes
Cooking Time: 1 and a ½ to 2 hours
Serving: 5
Preferred Wood Chip: Cherry

Ingredients:

- 1 cup of sriracha
- ½ a cup of butter
- ½ a cup of molasses
- ½ a cup of ketchup
- ¼ cup of firmly packed brown sugar
- ¼ cup of prepared yellow mustard
- 1 teaspoon of salt
- 1 teaspoon of freshly ground black pepper
- 1 whole chicken, cut into pieces
- ½ a teaspoon of freshly chopped parsley leaves

Directions:

1. Pre-heat your smoker to 250 degree Fahrenheit using cherry wood
2. Take a medium saucepan and place it over low heat, stir in butter, sriracha, ketchup, molasses, brown sugar, mustard, pepper and salt and keep stirring until the sugar and salt dissolves
3. Divide the sauce into two portions
4. Brush the chicken half with the sauce and reserve the remaining for serving
5. Make sure to keep the sauce for serving on the side, and keep the other portion for basting
6. Transfer chicken to your smoker rack and smoke for about 1 and a ½ to 2 hours until the internal temperature reaches 165 degree Fahrenheit
7. Sprinkle chicken with parsley and serve with reserved BBQ sauce
8. Enjoy!

Nutrition Value:

Calories: 148
Fats: 0.6g
Carbs: 10g
Fiber: 1g

38. SPICY JAMAICAN JERK

Preparation Time: 15 minutes
Cooking Time: 1 and a ½ hours
Serving: 4
Preferred Wood Chip: Mesquite

Ingredients:

- 4 chicken leg quarters
- ¼ cup of canola oil
- ¼ cup of cane syrup
- 8 whole cloves
- 6 sliced habanero peppers
- 1 chopped scallions, white and green parts
- 2 tablespoon of whole all spice berries
- 2 tablespoon of salt
- 2 teaspoon of freshly ground black pepper
- 2 teaspoon of ground cinnamon
- 1 teaspoon of cayenne pepper
- 1 teaspoon of dried thyme
- 1 teaspoon of ground cumin

Directions:

1. Pre-heat your smoker to 275 degree Fahrenheit with mesquite wood
2. Add a handful of whole all spice berries as well
3. Brush the chicken carefully with canola oil
4. Take a blender and add cane syrup, cloves, scallions, habaneros, salt, allspice, pepper, cinnamon, thyme, cayenne, cumin and pulse the whole mixture until you have a smooth and sticky texture
5. Keep 2 tablespoon of the mixture on the side
6. Brush the chicken with remaining mix thoroughly

7. Transfer to smoker rack and smoke for 1 and a ½ hours
8. Remove the chicken from smoker once done and let it rest for 10 minutes
9. Baste with more jerk seasoning and serve!

Nutrition Value:

Calories: 206
Fats: 2g
Carbs: 20g
Fiber: 1g

39. SUPREMELY SMOKED ALDERWOOD TURKEY BREAST

Preparation Time: 20 minutes + Overnight marinating time
Cooking Time: 3 and a ½ to 4 hours
Serving: 4
Preferred Wood Chip: Apple

Ingredients:

- 4 tablespoon of unsalted butter
- 8 teaspoon of Dijon mustard
- 2 tablespoon of chopped fresh thyme leaves
- 1 teaspoon of freshly ground black pepper
- ½ a teaspoon of kosher salt
- 1 bone-in turkey breast

Directions:

1. Take a small sized bowl and stir in butter, thyme, mustard, ¼ teaspoon of pepper, salt
2. Rub the turkey breast with the butter mix
3. Cover and allow it to refrigerate overnight
4. Pre-heat your smoker to 250 degree Fahrenheit using Apple wood chips
5. Sprinkle breast with ¾ teaspoon of pepper and transfer to smoker rack
6. Cover and smoke for 3 and a ½ to 4 hours, making sure to keep adding more chips after every 60 minutes
7. Once the internal temperature reaches 165 degree

Fahrenheit, remove the turkey and allow it to rest
8. Slice and serve!

Nutrition Value:

Calories: 238
Fats: 11g
Carbs: 40g
Fiber: 1g

40. CUTE PLUM CHICKEN POPS

Preparation Time: 35 minutes
Cooking Time: 2 hours
Serving: 8
Preferred Wood Chip: Cherry

Ingredients:

- 12 chicken drumsticks
- 2 teaspoon of salt
- 2 teaspoon of fresh ground black pepper
- Plum sauce (homemade or store bought)

Directions:

1. Pre-heat your smoker to 250 degree Fahrenheit using Cherry wood
2. Stretch the skin away from drumsticks as much as possible
3. Remove the tendons from each leg
4. Season the drumsticks with salt and pepper and transfer to your smoker rack
5. Smoker for 1 and a ½ hours
6. Baste the pops with plum sauce and transfer to smoker again, smoker for 30 minutes until the internal temperature reaches 165 degree Fahrenheit
7. Allow them to rest for a while
8. Coat the meat with more sauce and enjoy!

Nutrition Value:

Calories: 222
Fats: 11g
Carbs: 16g

Fiber: 3g

41. SMOKE WHOLE CHICKEN

Preparation Time: 4 hours 10 minutes
Servings: 4

Ingredients:

- 2 lbs whole chicken, rinse and trim
- 3 tbsp dry rub

Directions:

1. Preheat the smoker to 250 F/121 C using oak wood.
2. Tie chicken legs together using kitchen string.
3. Coat chicken well with dry rub.
4. Place chicken in smoker and smoke until internal temperature reaches 165 F/73 C about 3-4 hours.
5. Cut into the slices and serve.

Nutritional Values:
Calories 442
Fat 16.8 g
Carbohydrates 2.3 g
Sugar 0 g
Protein 65.6 g

42. SMOKY WRAP CHICKEN BREASTS

Preparation Time: 5 hours 30 minutes
Servings: 6

Ingredients:

- 6 chicken breasts, skinless and boneless
- 18 bacon slices
- 3 tbsp chicken rub

For brine:

- 1/4 cup brown sugar
- 1/4 cup kosher salt

- 4 cups water

Directions:
1. Combine together all brine ingredients into the glass dish.
2. Place chicken into the dish and coat well.
3. Soak chicken about 2 hours.
4. Rinse chicken well and coat with chicken rub.
5. Wrap each chicken breast with three bacon slices.
6. Preheat the smoker to 230 F/110 C using soaked wood chips.
7. Place wrapped chicken breasts into the smoker and smoke for about 3 hours or until internal temperature reaches 165 F/73 C.
8. Serve and enjoy.

Nutritional Values:
Calories 454
Fat 14.4 g
Carbohydrates 8.9 g
Sugar 8.9 g
Protein 32.8 g
Cholesterol 101 mg

43. SMOKED CHIPOTLE CHICKEN WINGS

Preparation Time: 2 hours 40 minutes
Servings: 6

Ingredients:
- 5 1/2 lbs chicken wings
- 1/2 tbsp ground cumin
- 1 tbsp ground mustard
- 1 tbsp smoked paprika
- 1 1/2 tbsp chipotle ground pepper
- 2 tbsp brown sugar
- 1/2 tbsp salt

Directions:
1. Add all ingredients into the large zip lock bag and mix well

and place the bag into the refrigerator for 30 minutes.
2. Preheat the smoker to 250 F/121 C using wood chips.
3. Remove chicken from refrigerator and place in smoker and smoke for 2 hours.
4. Serve hot and enjoy.

Nutritional Values:

Calories 815
Fat 31.6 g
Carbohydrates 4.5 g
Sugar 3.2 g
Protein 121 g
Cholesterol 370 mg

44. DELICIOUS SMOKED PULLED CHICKEN

Preparation Time: 4 hours 10 minutes
Servings: 6

Ingredients:

- 3 lbs chicken
- 1/2 cup BBQ rub
- 1/2 cup butter

Directions:

1. In a bowl, combine together butter and 2 tbsp BBQ rub.
2. Rub butter mixture all over the chicken.
3. Sprinkle remaining BBQ rub over the chicken.
4. Using foil wrap the chicken well.
5. Preheat the smoker to 230 F/110 F using wood chips.
6. Place chicken in smoker and smoker for 3 1/2 hours or until internal temperature reaches 165 F/73 C.
7. Unwrap the chicken and smoke for another 30 minutes.
8. Using fork shred the chicken and serves.

Nutritional Values:

Calories 478
Fat 22.2 g
Carbohydrates 0 g
Sugar 0 g

Protein 65.9 g
Cholesterol 215 mg

45. SMOKED CHICKEN THIGHS

Preparation Time: 4 hours 10 minutes
Servings: 6

Ingredients:

- 24 oz chicken thighs, skin on
- 2 tbsp black pepper
- 2 tbsp cayenne
- 1 tbsp garlic powder
- 1 tbsp thyme
- 2 tbsp chili powder
- 2 tbsp paprika
- 1 cup olive oil
- 1 tbsp salt

Directions:

1. Preheat the smoker to 200 F/93 C using wood chips.
2. Combine all dry seasoning ingredients together.
3. Coat chicken with olive oil then sprinkles seasoning over the chicken.
4. Place chicken in smoker and smoke for 2 hours.
5. After 2 hours flip the chicken and smoker for another 2 hours or until internal temperature reaches 165 F/73 C.
6. Serve and enjoy.

Nutritional Values:

Calories 535
Fat 43.1 g
Carbohydrates 6.3 g
Sugar 1 g
Protein 34.2 g
Cholesterol 101 mg

46. SIMPLE TURKEY BREAST

Preparation Time: 5 hours 5 minutes
Servings: 8

Ingredients:

- 5 lbs turkey breast
- 1/2 cup chicken rub seasoning

Directions:

1. Preheat the smoker to 225 F/107 C using wood chips.
2. Wash turkey and pat dry using a paper towel.
3. Rub chicken seasoning over the turkey and place in smoker.
4. Smoke turkey about 5 hours or until internal temperature reaches 165 F/73 C.
5. Serve and enjoy.

Nutritional Values:

Calories 310
Fat 5 g
Carbohydrates 14.9 g
Sugar 11 g
Protein 48.9 g
Cholesterol 122 mg

47. TASTY SMOKED CHICKEN TENDERS

Preparation Time: 1 hour 10 minutes
Servings: 8

Ingredients:

- 4 lbs chicken tenders, rinsed and pat dry
- 1/4 Tsp Cajun seasoning
- 3/4 Tsp fresh ginger, grated
- 2 tsp garlic, minced
- 1 1/2 tbsp sesame seeds
- 1/4 cup water
- 1/2 cup olive oil
- 1/2 cup soy sauce

Directions:

1. Add all ingredients into the zip lock bag and mix well and place in refrigerator for overnight.
2. Preheat the smoker to 225 F/107 C using wood chips.
3. Remove chicken tenders from marinade and place on middle rack of smoker and smoke for 1 hour or until internal temperature reaches 165 F/73 C.
4. Serve and enjoy.

Nutritional Values:

Calories 559
Fat 30.3 g
Carbohydrates 2 g
Sugar 0.3 g
Protein 67 g
Cholesterol 202 mg

48. CAJUN SEASONED CHICKEN BREAST

Preparation Time: 4 hours 10 minutes
Servings: 4

Ingredients:
- 2 lbs chicken breasts, boneless
- 1 cup BBQ sauce
- 2 tbsp Cajun seasoning

Directions:
1. Preheat the smoker to 225 F/107 C using apple wood chips.
2. Rub chicken with Cajun seasoning and place on the smoker rack and smoke for 4 hours or until internal temperature reaches 165 F/73 C.
3. Coat chicken with BBQ sauce during the last hour of cooking.
4. Serve and enjoy.

Nutritional Values:

Calories 525
Fat 17 g
Carbohydrates 22.7 g
Sugar 16.3 g

Protein 65.7 g
Cholesterol 202 mg

49. ORANGE SMOKED CHICKEN

Preparation Time: 2 hours 10 minutes
Servings: 3

Ingredients:

- 12 oz chicken breasts, rinse and trim excess fat

For rub:

- 2 tbsp chicken rub seasoning

For marinade:

- 1 tbsp garlic powder
- 1/2 cup soy sauce
- 2 cups orange juice

Directions:

1. Add chicken and marinade ingredients into the zip lock bag and mix well.
2. Place chicken bag in the refrigerator for overnight.
3. Preheat the smoker to 250 F/121 C using apple wood chips.
4. Remove chicken from marinade and rub chicken seasoning over the chicken.
5. Place chicken in smoker and smoker for 2 hours or until internal temperature reaches 165 F/73 C.
6. Serve and enjoy.

Nutritional Values:

Calories 322
Fat 8.8 g
Carbohydrates 22.5 g
Sugar 15.3 g
Protein 37.1 g
Cholesterol 101 mg

50. SMOKED SOY CHICKEN LEGS

Preparation Time: 4 hours 10 minutes

Servings: 4

Ingredients:

- 3 1/2 lbs chicken legs, rinse and pat dry
- 2 cups apple juice
- 1/4 cup BBQ spice
- 1/2 cup soy sauce
- 1/2 cup Italian salad dressing

Directions:

1. Add chicken, BBQ spice, soy sauce, and Italian salad dressing in zip lock bag and mix well.
2. Place chicken bag in the refrigerator for overnight.
3. Preheat the smoker to 250 F/121 C using apple wood.
4. Remove chicken from marinade and place in smoker and smoke for 4 hours.
5. After every 30 minutes misting with apple juice.
6. Serve and enjoy.

Nutritional Values:

Calories 928
Fat 37.9 g
Carbohydrates 23 g
Sugar 18.5 g
Protein 117 g
Cholesterol 373 mg

51. DELICIOUS HONEY SMOKED CHICKEN

Preparation Time: 2 hours 10 minutes
Servings: 4

Ingredients:

- 16 oz chicken breasts, skinless and boneless

For seasoning:

- 1 tsp onion powder
- 1 tsp garlic powder
- 1 tsp Chinese five spice

For marinade:

- 2 tbsp soy sauce
- 1/4 cup honey
- 3/4 cup orange juice

Directions:

1. Add all marinade ingredients into the microwave safe bowl and microwave for 30 seconds.
2. Add chicken and marinade into the zip lock bag and mix well.
3. Place marinated chicken in refrigerator for 1 hour.
4. Combine together all seasoning ingredients and set aside.
5. Preheat the smoker to 250 F/121 C using apple wood.
6. Remove chicken from marinade and sprinkle with seasoning mixture from both the sides.
7. Place chicken in smoker and smoke for 30 minutes then flip chicken and smoke for another 20 minutes or until internal temperature reaches 155 F/68 C.
8. Serve and enjoy.

Nutritional Values:

Calories 310
Fat 8.5 g
Carbohydrates 23.9 g
Sugar 21.8 g
Protein 33.9 g
Cholesterol 101 mg

52. SMOKED BUFFALO CHICKEN WINGS

Preparation Time: 4 hours 40 minutes
Servings: 8

Ingredients:

- 5 lbs chicken wings, rinse and pat dry
- Pepper
- Salt

For sauce:

- 2 tbsp butter
- 1 cup red hot sauce

Directions:

1. Place chicken wings into the refrigerator for 3 hours.
2. Preheat the smoker to 225 F/107 C.
3. Remove chicken wings from refrigerator and coat with little olive oil.
4. Season chicken wings with pepper and salt.
5. Place chicken wings in the smoker for 1 hour.
6. After 1-hour increase temperature to 350 F/176 C and smoke for another 30 minutes.
7. In a bowl, combine together sauce ingredients.
8. Add smoked chicken wings into the bowl and toss well.
9. Serve and enjoy.

Nutritional Values:

Calories 567
Fat 24 g
Carbohydrates 0.5 g
Sugar 0.4 g
Protein 82.2 g
Cholesterol 260 mg

53. MOIST WRAPPED CHICKEN TENDERS

Preparation Time: 40 minutes
Servings: 5

Ingredients:

- 1 lb chicken tenders
- 1 tbsp chili powder
- 1/3 cup brown sugar
- 1 tsp garlic powder
- 1 tsp onion powder
- 1 tsp paprika
- 1/2 Tsp Italian seasoning
- 10 bacon slices
- 1/2 Tsp pepper
- 1/2 Tsp salt

Directions:

1. Preheat the smoker to 350 F/176 C.
2. In a bowl, combine together Italian seasoning, garlic powder, onion powder, paprika, pepper, and salt.
3. Add chicken tenders to the bowl and toss well.
4. Wrap each chicken tenders with a bacon slice.
5. Mix together chili powder and brown sugar and sprinkle over the wrapped chicken.
6. Place wrapped the chicken in smoker and smoke for 30 minutes.
7. Serve and enjoy.

Nutritional Values:

Calories 247
Fat 7.9 g
Carbohydrates 11.5 g
Sugar 9.9 g
Protein 26.7 g
Cholesterol 81 mg

54. SWEET AND SPICY CHICKEN WINGS

Preparation Time: 1 hour 20 minutes
Servings: 8

Ingredients:

- 5 lbs chicken wings, rinsed and pat dry
- 3 tbsp apple juice
- 1/2 cup BBQ sauce
- 1 cup honey
- 1 tbsp garlic powder
- 1 tbsp chili powder
- 1 tbsp onion powder
- 2 1/2 tbsp ground black pepper
- 1 tbsp seasoned salt

Directions:

1. Combine together black pepper, seasoned salt, garlic powder, chili powder, and onion powder.
2. Add chicken wings into the zip lock bag then pour dry rub

mixture over the chicken and mix well.

3. Place chicken bag into the refrigerator for overnight.
4. Preheat the smoker to 225 F/107 C using apple wood chips.
5. Place chicken wings in smoker and smoke for 20 minutes.
6. After 20 minutes turn chicken and smoke for another 25 minutes or until internal temperature reach 165 F/73 C.
7. Meanwhile, in a small saucepan combine together BBQ sauce, honey, and apple juice and cook over medium heat.
8. Remove chicken wings from smoker and toss with BBQ sauce mixture.
9. Return chicken wings into the smoker and smoke for another 25 minutes.
10. Serve hot and enjoy.

Nutritional Values:

Calories 748
Fat 21.4 g
Carbohydrates 54.4 g
Sugar 48.5 g
Protein 82.8 g
Cholesterol 252 mg

55. SIMPLE SMOKED CHICKEN WINGS

Preparation Time: 1 hour 10 minutes
Servings: 8

Ingredients:

- 4 lbs chicken wings
- 1 bottle Italian dressing
- 3 tbsp chicken rub seasoning

Directions:

1. Add Italian dressing and chicken wings into the zip lock bag and place in refrigerator for overnight.
2. Drain chicken well and rub chicken seasoning over chicken wings.
3. Preheat the smoker to 300 F/148 C using apple wood.
4. Place coated chicken wings in the smoker and smoke for 1

hour.

5. Serve hot and enjoy.

Nutritional Values:

Calories 431
Fat 16.8 g
Carbohydrates 0 g
Sugar 0 g
Protein 65.6 g
Cholesterol 202 mg

56. SMOKED TURKEY

Preparation Time: 1 Hour 10 Minutes
Cooking Time: 4 Hours 20 Minutes
Servings: 5

Ingredients:

- 5 pounds turkey, trimmed with giblets removed
- 1 cup olive oil
- 5 tablespoons Ras el Hanout (Moroccan Spice Blend) seasoning
- Kosher salt, to taste
- Zest of 3 lemons
- Mint leaves for garnishing

Directions:

1. Cut the backbone of turkey and remove the spine and discard the fat.
2. Flip the turkey breast-side up and hand-press into the breastbone to flatten it.
3. Rub the turkey with oil and then massage the seasoning along with salt and lemon zest.
4. Cover the turkey with plastic wrap and marinate it for 30 minutes.
5. Preheat the smoker for 20 minutes.
6. Soak the wood chip in water one hour before smoking.
7. Remove plastic wrap and cook the turkey for 4 hours 20 minutes at 250 degrees F.

8. Garnish it with mint leaves.

Nutrition Values:

Calories 1062
Total Fat 72.7g
Saturated Fat 15.9g
Cholesterol 284mg
Sodium 1660mg
Total Carbohydrate 3.8g
Dietary Fiber 2.2g
Total Sugars 1.5g
Protein 85.2g
Calcium 45mg
Iron 1mg
Potassium 10mg

57. TURKEY WITH CHIMICHURRI

Preparation Time: 1 Hour 10 Minutes
Cooking Time: 4 Hours
Servings: 5

Ingredients:

- 5 pounds bone-in, skin on turkey pieces
- Salt and pepper
- 1teaspoon paprika
- ½ teaspoon cayenne
- 2 tablespoons olive oil
- 1 pepper
- 1 onion
- 2 carrots, chopped
- 2 scallions
- 2 tomatoes, chopped
- Homemade Chimichurri Sauce
- ½ cup olive oil
- 1 teaspoon parsley
- 1 teaspoon red pepper flakes
- 2 garlic cloves

- 2 red onions

Directions:
1. Season the washed and clean turkey with the salt, pepper, paprika and cayenne pepper.
2. Rub it gently all over.
3. Arrange the wood chip inside the smoker and then preheat the smoker to 230 degrees F.
4. Transfer the turkey to the sheet pan and arrange peppers, onions, carrots, scallion, and tomatoes beside it.
5. Drizzle the olive oil on top.
6. Place the pan sheet inside the smoker.
7. Close the electric smoker door and then cook for 4 hours at 250 degrees F.
8. Check the turkey to an internal temperature of 165°F.
9. Now, it is time to make the chimichurri.
10. Blend all the homemade chimichurri ingredients in a blender and puree until combined.
11. Serve the cooked turkey and veggie with the ready to serve the sauce.

Nutrition Values:
Calories 807
Total Fat 35.9g
Saturated Fat 4.5g
Cholesterol 283mg
Sodium 920mg
Total Carbohydrate 11.7g
Dietary Fiber 2.9g
Total Sugars 5.8g
Protein 94.8g
Calcium 32mg
Iron 6mg
Potassium 311mg

58. WHOLE SMOKED TURKEY RECIPE

Preparation Time: 16 Hours
Cooking Time: 10 Hours

Servings: 14

Ingredients:

- ½ cup salt
- ⅓ cup molasses
- ⅓ cup granulated sugar
- ½ cup Worcestershire sauce
- 6 cloves, smashed garlic
- 4 dried bay leaves
- Black pepper to taste
- 14 pounds whole turkey
- 2 cups bourbon
- 1 cup canola oil for coating

Directions:

1. Pour a gallon of water, salt, sugar, molasses, garlic, Worcestershire sauce, bourbon, pepper, and bay leaves in a large pot.
2. Boil it for a few minutes and then cool it down completely.
3. Submerge the turkey completely in the brine using a large bucket.
4. Brine it in the liquid for 15 hours.
5. The next day, take the turkey out of the brine and pat dry with paper towel.
6. Rub the turkey with oil and additional pepper.
7. Load the smoker with soaked wood chips, and place the turkey inside the smoker for cooking.
8. Set temperature to 250 degrees F.
9. Once the internal temperate is 165 degrees F, the turkey is ready.
10. Note: It took about 10 hours of cooking.

Nutrition Values:

Calories 770
Total Fat 29.2g
Saturated Fat 1.7g
Cholesterol 249mg
Sodium 9583mg 4
Total Carbohydrate 47.8g

Dietary Fiber 1.9g
Total Sugars 29g
Protein 61.3g
Calcium 95mg
Iron 10mg
Potassium 1705mg

59. CLASSIC SMOKED TURKEY RECIPE

Preparation Time: 30 Minutes
Cooking Time: 12 Hours
Servings: 16

Ingredients:

- 16 pounds turkey
- 2 tablespoons dried thyme
- 1 tablespoon dried sage
- 2 teaspoons dried oregano
- 2 teaspoons paprika
- 1 tablespoon sea salt
- Black pepper, to taste
- 1 teaspoon dried rosemary
- Zest of 1 orange
- ⅓ cup extra-virgin olive oil
- ⅓ cup apple cider
- ⅓ cups water

Directions:

1. Preheat the electric smoker to 250 degrees F.
2. Take a small bowl and mix all the dry spices and ingredients.
3. Rub it gently over the rekey meat.
4. At the end drizzle olive oil on top.
5. Now pour water along with apple cider in the large water pan in the bottom of the electric smoker.
6. Place a drip pan on the next rack or shelf of the smoker.
7. Fill the sides with the apple wood chips.
8. Place the turkey on the top rack of the smoker.
9. Close the door of the rack and then cook for approximately

12 hours.

10. Add more wood if smoke stops coming.
11. Use the digital probe thermometer to get an internal temperature of 165 degrees F.
12. Remove the turkey and serve.

Nutrition Values:

Calories 818
Total Fat 27g
Saturated Fat 8.1g
Cholesterol 343mg 1
Sodium 669mg
Total Carbohydrate 2.6g
Dietary Fiber 0.7g
Total Sugars 1.7g
Protein 133.1g
Calcium 31mg
Iron 46mg 2
Potassium 1393mg

60. TURKEY IN THE ELECTRIC SMOKER

Preparation Time: 1 Hour 10 Minutes
Cooking Time: 10 Hours
Servings: 10

Ingredients:

- 1 (10 pounds) whole turkey
- 4 cloves garlic, crushed
- 2 tablespoons salt, seasoned
- ½ cup butter
- 1 (12 fluid ounce) cola-flavored carbonated beverage
- 1 apple, quartered
- 1 onion, quartered
- 1 tablespoon garlic powder
- 1 tablespoon salt
- 1 tablespoon black pepper

Directions:

1. Preheat your electric smoker to 225 degrees F and then rinse the turkey well under water, pat dry and then rub it with seasoned salt.
2. Place it inside a roasting pan.
3. Combine cola, butter, apples, garlic powder, salt, and pepper in a bowl .
4. Fill the cavity of turkey with cola, apples, garlic powder, salt, and pepper.
5. Rub butter and crushed garlic outside of the turkey as well.
6. Cover the turkey with foil.
7. Smoke the turkey for 10 hours at 250 degrees F.
8. Once it's done, serve.

Nutrition Values:

Calories 907
Total Fat 63.2g
Saturated Fat 22.3g 1
Cholesterol 4256mg 14
Sodium 2364mg 1
Total Carbohydrate 17.9g
Dietary Fiber 1.1g
Total Sugars 9.7g
Protein 62.7g
Calcium 462mg
Iron 19mg 1
Potassium 710mg

SEAFOOD

61. SIMPLE SALT & PEPPER SMOKED SALMON

Preparation Time: 40 Minutes
Cooking Time: 2 Hours
Servings: 2

Ingredients:

- 2 pounds fresh salmon fillets

- 4 tablespoons melted butter
- 2 tablespoons lemon juice
- Salt and pepper

Directions:

1. Preheat the smoker to 225 degrees F.
2. Add wood chips to begin the smoke.
3. Now brush the butter over the fillets.
4. Pour lemon juice over the fillets.
5. Sprinkle the generous amount of pepper and salt to taste.
6. Place salmon into the electric smoker.
7. Cook for 2 hours.
8. Once the fillets temperature reaches 150 degrees Fahrenheit, it's done.
9. Serve and enjoy.

Nutrition Values:

Calories 807
Total Fat 51.2g
Saturated Fat 18.7g
Cholesterol 261mg
Sodium 367mg
Total Carbohydrate 0.4g
Dietary Fiber 0.1g
Total Sugars 0.3g
Protein 88.4g
Calcium 168mg
Iron 3mg
Potassium 1768mg

62. SMOKED FISH IN A BRINE

Preparation Time: 12 Hours
Cooking Time: 5 Hours
Servings: 5

Ingredients:

- 5 pounds of fish fillets
- BRINE Ingredients:

- 1 gallon water
- 2 cups canning salt
- ⅔ cup brown sugar

Directions:

1. Combine sugar, water, and salt in a large pot.
2. Split the fish into two halves and then soaks in the brine overnight.
3. Prepare the electric smoker and then use apple wood chip to create smoke.
4. Place the fish for cooking inside the smoker and let it cook for 5 hours at 225 degrees F.
5. The time depends on the temperature of how hot the smoker gets.

Nutrition Values:

Calories 773
Total Fat 43.1g
Saturated Fat 0g
Cholesterol 0mg
Sodium 36892mg 16
Total Carbohydrate 24.3g
Dietary Fiber 0g
Total Sugars 18.8g
Protein 72.1g
Calcium 39mg
Iron 0mg
Potassium 33mg

63. CLASSIC SMOKE TROUT

Preparation Time: 30 Minutes
Cooking Time: 4 Hours
Servings: 2

Ingredients for The Brine

- 3 cups water
- 1-2 cups dark-brown sugar
- 1 cup of coarse salt

- Ingredients for The Trout
- 4 pounds of trout, backbone and pin bones removed
- 2 tablespoons vegetable oil for the grill basket

Directions:
1. First, make the brine by mixing all the brine Ingredients: in a large pot.
2. Submerge the fish in the brine for a few hours.
3. Then pat dry the fish and drizzle oil all over the fish.
4. Heat the smoker and add the wood chips.
5. Fill the water pan with water.
6. Wait until the smoke started to come out.
7. Place a dripping pan beneath the grill grate to get all the drippings.
8. Soak the wood in water and then add to coals.
9. Smoke the fish for 4 hours at 225 degrees F, then serve.

Nutrition Values:
Calories 1400
Total Fat 52g
Saturated Fat 9.4g
Cholesterol 336mg 1
Sodium 46425mg 20
Total Carbohydrate 107.9g
Dietary Fiber 0g
Total Sugars 106.7g
Protein 120.9g
Calcium 351mg
Iron 9mg
Potassium 2250mg

64. SMOKED SALMON

Preparation Time: 2 Hours
Cooking Time: 5 Hours
Servings: 5

Ingredients:
- 5 pounds salmon, trout or char

- 1 ½ cup of maple syrup for basting
- BRINE Ingredients:
- 1-quart cold water
- ⅓ cup Diamond Crystal kosher salt
- 1 cup brown sugar

Directions:

1. Combine brine ingredients in a large bowl and place fish in for 2 hours. Next, pat dry the fish and let it dry. Place the fish on a rack and smoke the fish at 225 degrees F for 5 hours.
2. After one hour of cooking, baste the chicken with the maple syrup repeat every one hour.
3. The internal temperature of fish should be about 140°F to 150 degrees F.
4. The smoked fish is ready to be served. Enjoy.

Nutrition Values:

Calories 725
Total Fat 10.7g
Saturated Fat 2.2g
Cholesterol 250mg
Sodium 8141mg 3
Total Carbohydrate 70.7g
Dietary Fiber 0g
Total Sugars 65.6g
Protein 89.3g
Calcium 107mg
Iron 3mg
Potassium 1816mg

65. SMOKED FISH WITH THE DELICIOUS DIP

Preparation Time: 3 Hours
Cooking Time: 6 Hours
Servings: 6

Brine Ingredients:

- 1-quart cold water

- ⅓ cup salt
- 1 cup brown sugar
- ½ cup soy sauce
- ½ cup of vinegar

Ingredients for Sauce:

- ½ cup almond milk
- 6 ounces cream cheese, softened
- ⅓ cup finely minced onion
- ½ stalk celery, finely chopped
- 1 tablespoon minced fresh parsley
- ½ teaspoon lemon juice
- 1 teaspoon Worcestershire sauce
- Cayenne pepper, to taste
- Salt and black pepper to taste
- Other Ingredients:
- 6 pounds of fish fillet

Directions:

1. Combine the brine ingredients in a large bowl and place the fish in the brine for 2 hours.
2. Next, blend all the sauce ingredients in a blender to make a smooth paste.
3. Next, pat dries the fish with paper towel. Place the fish on a topmost rack of the smoker and smoke the fish at 225 degrees F for 6 hours.
4. The internal temperature of fish should be about 150°F once done the cooking.
5. Enjoy warm served with prepared sauce.

Nutrition Values:

Calories 1268
Total Fat 65.9g
Saturated Fat 19g
Cholesterol 185mg
Sodium 10012mg 4
Total Carbohydrate 104.8g
Dietary Fiber 2.6g

Total Sugars 24.9g
Protein 70.2g
Calcium 137mg
Iron 11mg
Potassium 1597mg

66. HONEY MUSTARD HALIBUT FILLETS

Preparation Time: 3 Hours
Cooking Time: 6 Hours
Servings: 6

Brine Ingredients:

1. ⅓ cup kosher salt
2. 1 cup brown sugar
3. 4 tablespoons cumin
4. 1 tablespoon dried bay leaves, crushed
5. ½ gallon water
6. Other Ingredients:
7. 6 halibut fillets
8. 1 cup honey mustard rub

Directions:

1. Combine and mix well all the brine ingredients in a large bowl and place the fish in it for 2 hours. Next, pat dry the fish and let it dry. Season the fish with the mustard rub and massage gently for fine coating.
2. Place the fish on a rack inside the smoker and cook for 6 hours at 225 degrees F.
3. The internal temperature of fish should be about 150°F at the end of cooking.
4. Serve and enjoy.

Nutrition Values:

Calories 456
Total Fat 9.6g
Saturated Fat 1.5g
Cholesterol 101mg
Sodium 6592mg 2
Total Carbohydrate 27.1g

Dietary Fiber 0.5g
Total Sugars 23.8g
Protein 63.1g
Calcium 90mg
Iron 16mg
Potassium 1416mg

67. PINEAPPLE MAPLE GLAZE FISH IN THE SMOKER

Preparation Time: 3 Hours
Cooking Time: 6 Hours
Servings: 6

Ingredients:

- 6 pounds fresh salmon
- ⅓ cup maple syrup
- ½ cup pineapple juice

Brine Ingredients:

- ½ gallon water
- ⅓ cup sea salt (non-iodized)
- 1 cup pineapple juice
- ¼ cup brown sugar
- 3 tablespoons Worcestershire sauce
- 2 tablespoons garlic salt

Directions:

1. Prepare the brine by mixing all the brine ingredients in a large pot. Submerge the fish in it for 2 hours. Next, pat dry the fish and let it dry.
2. Preheat the smoker to 225 degrees F.
3. Place the dry salmon inside the smoker once the smoker starts to build.
4. Place the fish in the smoker and cook it for 6 hours.
5. Now mix ½ cup pineapple juice with maple syrup and baste the fish every 30 minutes, while cooking.
6. Add soaked wood chip if the smoke is not enough.
7. Serve it once done.

Nutrition Values: 6

Calories 708
Total Fat 28.1g
Saturated Fat 4g
Cholesterol 200mg
Sodium 5289mg 2
Total Carbohydrate 26.6g
Dietary Fiber 0.4g
Total Sugars 22.6g
Protein 88.6g
Calcium 194mg
Iron 3mg
Potassium 1874mg

68. SMOKED TUNA

Preparation Time: 12 Hours
Cooking Time: 90 Minutes
Servings: 2

Ingredients for The Tuna:

- 2 pounds tuna steaks
- 2 tablespoons soy sauce
- Ingredients for The Brine:
- 6-10 cups warm water
- ½ cup salt

Dip Ingredients:

- ½ cup mayonnaise
- 2 ounces cream cheese
- ½ cup red onion, diced
- ⅓ cup fresh parsley, chopped
- 3 tablespoons lemon juice
- ½ tablespoon garlic powder
- ⅓ teaspoon black pepper
- Salt, to taste
- ½ tablespoon hot sauce

Directions:

1. Prepare brine by combining the entire brine ingredient in a pot.
2. Soak the tuna in the brine overnight.
3. Water should be enough to cover the tune well.
4. Afterward, rinse under tap water.
5. Pat dry the tuna with the paper towel, and then let it sit at room temperate to get dry.
6. Rinse, dry, and lightly coat with soy sauce.
7. Preheat the smoker and cook the tuna inside a smoker at 250 degrees F for 90 minutes.
8. Meanwhile, prepare the sauce by mixing together the entire dip ingredient in a small bowl.
9. Remove the tuna from smoker and let it get cold. Chop the tuna if desired.
10. Add chopped tuna to the dip and let it sit in a refrigerator for a few minutes.
11. Then serve.

Nutrition Values:

Calories 1200
Total Fat 58.3g
Saturated Fat 16.6g
Cholesterol 269mg
Sodium 30031mg 13
Total Carbohydrate 21.6g
Dietary Fiber 1.5g
Total Sugars 6.4g
Protein 140.6g
Calcium 122mg
Iron 8mg
Potassium 1703mg

69. SMOKED EEL

Preparation Time: 12 Hours
Cooking Time: 3 Hours
Servings: 2

Ingredients for Brine:

- 10 cups warm water
- 1-½ cup salt
- ½ cup brown sugar
- 4 lemons, halved
- 2 sprigs fresh thyme

Other Ingredients:
- 2 fillets whole eel, cleaned and washed

Directions:
1. First, prepare the brine by mixing all the brine ingredients in a large pot, and place eel in it for 10 hours. Next day, pat dry the eel and let it dry.
2. Now, preheat the electric smoker to 235 degrees F and add wood chips.
3. Smoke the eel for about 3 hours.
4. Once the skins get crisp, the eel is ready to be served.
5. Enjoy.

Nutrition Values:
Calories 549
Total Fat 24.2g
Saturated Fat 4.9g
Cholesterol 256mg
Sodium 56739mg 24
Total Carbohydrate 47g
Dietary Fiber 3.6g
Total Sugars 38.1g
Protein 39g
Calcium 191mg
Iron 4mg
Potassium 795mg

70. SMOKED CATFISH RECIPE

Preparation Time: 3 Hours
Cooking Time: 5 Hours
Servings: 5

Ingredients for The Rub:

- 3 tablespoons paprika
- ½ teaspoon salt
- 2 tablespoons garlic powder
- 2 tablespoons onion powder
- ⅓ tablespoon dried thyme
- ⅓ tablespoon cayenne
- Other Ingredients:
- 5 fresh catfish fillets, about 1 pound each
- 4 tablespoons butter, soften

Directions:

1. Mix all rub ingredients in a small bowl.
2. Lightly rub the fillets with butter.
3. Sprinkle the generous amount of rub onto fillets.
4. Preheat the smoker to 225 degrees F,and add wood chips.
5. Once the smoker starts to smoke, place the fish inside the smoker.
6. Cook for 5 hours.
7. Then serve.

Nutrition Values:

Calories 332
Total Fat 22g
Saturated Fat 8.2g
Cholesterol 100mg
Sodium 387mg
Total Carbohydrate 7.3g
Dietary Fiber 2.2g
Total Sugars 2.3g
Protein 26.5g
Calcium 41mg
Iron 3mg
Potassium 685mg

71. BASIC BRISKET

Servings: 12

Preparation time: 45 minutes
Cooking time: 8 to 9 hours plus 1 to 2 hours resting

Ingredients :

- 1 full "whole packer" beef brisket (12 to 15 pounds)
- 1/2 cup brown sugar (divided)
- 1/4 cup chili powder
- 1/4 cup sweet paprika
- 1/4 cup kosher salt, plus more to taste
- 2 tablespoons garlic powder
- 2 tablespoons onion powder
- 2 tablespoons ground cumin
- 1 tablespoon ancho chili powder
- 1 tablespoon freshly ground black pepper, plus more to taste
- 1 teaspoon cayenne pepper, plus more to taste
- 4 tablespoons butter (melted)

Directions:

1. Pour 2 cups water into the Masterbuilt smoker's water pan. Place a mixture of hickory and apple wood chips in the smoker's wood tray and preheat smoker to 250°F.
2. Thoroughly rinse brisket with cold water and pat dry with paper towels. Trim brisket as necessary to about 1/4" fat and trim fat between the flat and the deckle (separate portions if necessary to fit in smoker).
3. Mix 1/4 cup brown sugar with chili powder, paprika, salt, garlic powder, onion powder, cumin, ancho chili powder, black pepper and cayenne pepper and rub all over brisket.
4. Place brisket fat-side down on smoker grate and smoke until the internal temperature of the meat reaches 165°F, about 6 hours. Add wood chips to the wood tray as necessary.
5. Mix butter and remaining 1/4 cup brown sugar and brush all over brisket. Wrap brisket in two layers of aluminum foil and continue smoking until the internal temperature of the meat reaches 200°F, 2 to 3 hours more.
6. Remove brisket from smoker and let rest for 1 to 2 hours. Slice brisket against the grain and serve with barbecue sauce

as desired. Enjoy!

Nutrition Values:

Calories: 358; Total Fat: 23g; Saturated Fat: 11g; Protein: 29g; Carbs: 9g; Fiber: 2g; Sugar: 4g

72. CENTRAL TEXAS-STYLE BRISKET

Servings: 12
Preparation time: 45 minutes
Cooking time: 8 to 9 hours plus 1 to 2 hours resting

Ingredients :

- 1 full "whole packer" beef brisket (12 to 15 pounds)
- 1/2 cup kosher salt, plus more to taste
- 1/2 cup black pepper, plus more to taste
- 2 teaspoons onion powder
- 1 tablespoon garlic powder

Directions:

1. Pour 2 cups water into the Masterbuilt smoker's water pan. Place mesquite wood chips in the smoker's wood tray and preheat smoker to 250°F.
2. Thoroughly rinse brisket with cold water and pat dry with paper towels. Trim brisket as necessary to about 1/4" fat and trim fat between the flat and the deckle (separate portions if necessary to fit in smoker).
3. Mix salt, pepper, onion powder and garlic powder and rub all over brisket.
4. Place brisket fat-side down on smoker grate and smoke until the internal temperature of the meat reaches 165°F, about 6 hours. Add wood chips to the wood tray as necessary.
5. Wrap brisket in two layers of aluminum foil and continue smoking until the internal temperature of the meat reaches 200°F, 2 to 3 hours more. Add wood chips to the wood tray as necessary.
6. Remove brisket from smoker and let rest for 1 to 2 hours. Slice brisket against the grain and serve. Enjoy!

Nutrition Values:

Calories: 315; Total Fat: 20g; Saturated Fat: 8g; Protein: 29g; Carbs: 5g; Fiber: 2g; Sugar: 0g

73. KANSAS CITY BRISKET SANDWICHES

Servings: 16
Preparation time: 1 hour
Cooking time: 8 to 9 hours
If you have the time and frying experience, substitute a batch of homemade beer-battered onion rings for the frozen package in this recipe.

Ingredients :

- 1 full "whole packer" beef brisket (12 to 15 pounds)
- 3 tablespoons kosher salt, plus more to taste
- 2 tablespoons freshly ground black pepper, plus more to taste
- 2 tablespoons garlic powder
- 2 tablespoons onion powder
- 1 tablespoon ground mustard
- 1 teaspoon cayenne pepper, plus more to taste
- 1 package (12 to 14 ounces) frozen beer battered onion rings
- 16 Kaiser rolls
- 4 tablespoons butter (softened)
- 16 deli slices provolone cheese
- 1 bottle (18 ounces) KC Masterpiece barbecue sauce

Directions:

1. Pour 2 cups water into the Masterbuilt smoker's water pan. Place hickory or cherry wood chips in the smoker's wood tray and preheat smoker to 250°F.
2. Thoroughly rinse brisket with cold water and pat dry with paper towels. Trim brisket as necessary to about 1/4" fat and trim fat between the flat and the deckle (separate portions if necessary to fit in smoker).

3. Mix salt, pepper, garlic powder, onion powder, ground mustard and cayenne pepper and rub all over brisket.
4. Place brisket fat-side down on smoker grate and smoke until the internal temperature of the meat reaches 180°F, about 7 hours. Add wood chips to the wood tray as necessary.
5. Cover brisket with aluminum foil and continue smoking until the internal temperature of the meat reaches 200°F, 1 to 2 hours more. Add wood chips to the wood tray as necessary.
6. Remove brisket from smoker, cover with aluminum foil and let rest while you prepare the frozen onion rings according to package directions, about 30 minutes.
7. Spread butter over cut surfaces of rolls and toast in preheated oven until golden, 7 to 8 minutes.
8. Thinly slice brisket against the grain and pile onto roll heels. Top meat with cheese slices, barbecue sauce and onion rings and serve immediately. Enjoy!

Nutrition Values:

Calories: 665; Total Fat: 35g; Saturated Fat: 17g; Protein: 35g; Carbs: 53g; Fiber: 3g; Sugar: 13g

74. KANSAS CITY BURNT ENDS

Servings: 6
Preparation time: 1 hour
Cooking time: 6 to 7 hours
The thick, sweet and smoky sauce in this recipe is a Kansas City-style treat!

Ingredients :
- 1 brisket point (4 to 5 pounds)
- 1/2 cup brown sugar
- 1/2 cup white sugar
- 1/4 cup kosher salt, plus more to taste
- 1/4 cup chili powder
- 1/4 cup coarsely ground black pepper, plus more to taste
- 3 tablespoons paprika
- 3 tablespoons ground cumin

- 2 teaspoons cayenne pepper, plus more to taste
- 1 tablespoon garlic powder
- 1 tablespoon onion powder
- 1 tablespoon butter
- 1/4 cup minced onion
- 4 garlic cloves (minced)
- 1 cup ketchup
- 1 cup tomato sauce
- 3/4 cup red wine vinegar
- 1/4 cup molasses
- 1 teaspoon hickory-flavored liquid smoke, plus more to taste
- Dash cinnamon or ginger

Directions:

1. Pour 2 cups water into the Masterbuilt smoker's water pan. Place hickory or cherry wood chips in the smoker's wood tray and preheat smoker to 225°F.
2. Thoroughly rinse brisket point with cold water, pat dry with paper towels and trim fat to 1/4". Mix brown sugar, white sugar, salt, chili powder, black pepper, paprika, cumin and cayenne pepper. Set aside about 1/3 of the spice mixture to make the sauce. Add garlic powder and onion powder to remaining spice mixture and rub over brisket.
3. Place brisket fat-side down on smoker grate and smoke until the internal temperature of the meat reaches 175°F, about 5 hours. Add wood chips to the wood tray as necessary.
4. Wrap brisket in aluminum foil and continue smoking until the internal temperature of the meat reaches 200°F, 1 to 2 hours more. Add wood chips to the wood tray as necessary.
5. Meanwhile, for the sauce, melt butter in a medium saucepan over medium-low heat and sauté onion until tender, about 5 minutes, stirring frequently. Add garlic and sauté about 1 minute more, stirring constantly. Add ketchup, tomato sauce, vinegar, molasses, liquid smoke and reserved spice mixture and season to taste with salt and pepper. Heat sauce to a boil, stirring occasionally. Reduce heat and simmer to thicken to desired consistency, stirring occasionally, 10 to 15 minutes.

6. Remove wrapped brisket from smoker and let rest for about 30 minutes. Remove foil from brisket, saving the cooking juices. Chop brisket into 1" chunks and toss with the cooking juices. Serve burnt ends with the sauce and enjoy!

Nutrition Values:

Calories: 432; Total Fat: 22g; Saturated Fat: 9g; Protein: 30g; Carbs: 29g; Fiber: 3g; Sugar: 19g

75. PRIME RIB

Servings: 8
Preparation time: 30 minutes
Cooking time: 5 1/2 hours

Ingredients :

- 1 prime rib roast (about 8 pounds)
- 2 tablespoons horseradish mustard
- 2 tablespoons peppercorns
- 1 tablespoon kosher salt
- 2 teaspoons dried rosemary
- 2 teaspoons dried thyme
- 1 teaspoon white sugar
- 1/2 teaspoon red pepper flakes

Directions:

1. Pour about 2 cups water into the Masterbuilt smoker's water pan. Place hickory wood chips in the smoker's wood tray and preheat smoker to 225°F.
2. Trim roast with a sharp knife as necessary to about 1/4" fat. Tie roast in a roll shape with kitchen twine. Rub roast all over with mustard. Pulse peppercorns, salt, rosemary, thyme, sugar and red pepper flakes in a food processor or spice grinder and rub all over roast. (If desired, refrigerate roast, uncovered, for up to 8 hours).
3. Place roast fat-side up on smoker grate and smoke until the internal temperature of the meat reaches 135°F, about 5 1/2 hours for a medium-rare roast (reduce smoking time for a rare roast). Add wood chips to the wood tray as necessary.

4. Remove roast from smoker, cover loosely with aluminum foil and let rest for about 30 minutes. Slice roast as desired and serve. Enjoy!

Nutrition Values:

Calories: 249; Total Fat: 11g; Saturated Fat: 4g; Protein: 47g; Carbs: 0g; Fiber: 0g; Sugar: 0g

76. SANTA MARIA SIRLOIN TIP ROAST

Servings: 6
Preparation time: 30 minutes
Cooking time: 2 1/2 hours

Ingredients :

- 1 sirloin tip roast (about 3 pounds)
- 1/4 cup olive oil (divided)
- 2 tablespoons kosher salt, plus more to taste
- 1 teaspoon coarsely ground black pepper, plus more to taste
- 1 teaspoon garlic powder

Directions:

1. Pour about 2 cups water into the Masterbuilt smoker's water pan. Place red oak or oak wood chips in the smoker's wood tray and preheat smoker to 250°F.
2. Brush roast all over with 2 tablespoons olive oil. Mix salt, pepper and garlic powder and rub all over roast. Heat remaining 2 tablespoons olive oil in a large nonstick skillet and sear until browned on all sides, turning as necessary, about 8 minutes.
3. Place roast on smoker grate and smoke until the internal temperature of the meat reaches 145°F, about 2 1/2 hours for a medium-rare roast (reduce smoking time for a rare roast). Add wood chips to the wood tray as necessary.
4. Remove roast from smoker, cover loosely with aluminum foil and let rest for about 10 minutes. Slice roast as desired and serve. Enjoy!

Nutrition Values:

Calories: 260; Total Fat: 10g; Saturated Fat: 4g; Protein: 41g; Carbs: 0g; Fiber: 0g; Sugar: 0g

77. SANTA CLARA TRI-TIP ROAST

Servings: 6
Preparation time: 15 minutes
Cooking time: 1 1/2 hours

Ingredients :

- 1 tri-tip roast (about 2 1/2 pounds)
- 2 tablespoons olive oil
- 2 teaspoons kosher salt, plus more to taste
- 2 teaspoons freshly ground black pepper
- 1 teaspoon garlic salt
- 1 teaspoon dried parsley

Directions:

1. Pour about 2 cups water into the Masterbuilt smoker's water pan. Place red oak or oak wood chips in the smoker's wood tray and preheat smoker to 250°F.
2. Remove silver skin from roast if necessary and brush roast with olive oil. Mix salt, pepper and garlic powder and rub all over roast.
3. Place roast on smoker grate and smoke until the internal temperature of the meat reaches 130°F, about 1 1/2 hours.
4. Remove roast from smoker, wrap tightly with aluminum foil and let rest for about 20 minutes. Cut roast against the grain into 1/4" thick slices and serve. Enjoy!

Nutrition Values:

Calories: 471; Total Fat: 24g; Saturated Fat: 8g; Protein: 63g; Carbs: 00g; Fiber: 0g; Sugar: 0g

78. BEEF SHORT RIBS

Servings: 6
Preparation time: 45 minutes

Cooking time: 5 to 6 hours

Ingredients :

- 12 beef short ribs (about 6 pounds, about 5" long)
- 1 cup yellow mustard
- 2 tablespoons soy sauce
- 2 tablespoons apple cider vinegar
- 1 tablespoon lime juice
- 2 tablespoons kosher salt, plus more to taste
- 2 tablespoons freshly ground black pepper, plus more to taste
- 2 tablespoons brown sugar
- 2 tablespoons garlic powder
- 1 tablespoon sweet paprika

Directions:

1. Pour about 2 cups water into the Masterbuilt smoker's water pan. Place pecan or cherry wood chips in the smoker's wood tray and preheat smoker to 225°F.
2. Remove silver skin from ribs if necessary, trim fat if desired and score ribs along the bones with a sharp knife. Mix mustard, soy sauce, vinegar and lime juice and rub all over ribs. Mix salt, pepper, brown sugar, garlic powder and paprika and rub all over ribs. Let ribs stand for about 15 minutes.
3. Place ribs bone-sides down on smoker grate and smoke until tender and the internal temperature of the meat reaches 190°F, 5 to 6 hours. Add wood chips to the wood tray as necessary.
4. Remove ribs from smoker, cover loosely with aluminum foil and let rest for about 15 minutes. Cut ribs into individual pieces and serve with barbecue sauce if desired. Enjoy!

Nutrition Values:

Calories: 284; Total Fat: 16 g; Saturated Fat: 7g; Protein: 31g; Carbs: 5g; Fiber: 1g Sugar: 3g

79. SHORT RIBS TEXAS-STYLE

Servings: 6
Preparation time: 45 minutes plus 12 to 24 hours refrigeration
Cooking time: 6 to 7 hours

Ingredients :

- 12 beef short ribs (about 6 pounds, about 5" long)
- 1/3 cup kosher salt (divided)
- 3 tablespoons coarsely ground black pepper
- 2 tablespoons paprika
- 2 tablespoon chili powder
- 1 tablespoon cayenne pepper, plus more to taste
- 1 tablespoon garlic powder
- 1 tablespoon onion powder
- 1 cup beef broth
- 1/2 cup butter (melted)

Directions:

1. Remove silver skin from ribs if necessary and trim fat. Using a sharp knife, cut ribs into portions with 2 bones each. Rub ribs all over with about 1 tablespoon salt, place in a covered container and refrigerate for 12 to 24 hours.
2. Pour about 2 cups water into the Masterbuilt smoker's water pan. Place oak or hickory wood chips in the smoker's wood tray and preheat smoker to 225°F.
3. Mix remaining salt with pepper, paprika, chili powder, cayenne pepper, garlic powder and onion powder. Set aside about 2 tablespoons spice mixture. Rub remaining spice mixture all over ribs. Let ribs stand for about 15 minutes.
4. Place ribs bone-sides down on smoker grate and smoke for about 1 hour.
5. Mix reserved spice mixture, broth and butter and mop over ribs. Continue smoking until ribs are tender and the internal temperature of the meat reaches 200°F, 4 to 5 more hours mopping about every hour (briefly microwave mop sauce as

needed to re-melt the butter). Add wood chips to the wood tray as necessary.

6. Remove ribs from smoker, cover loosely with aluminum foil and let rest for about 15 minutes. Cut ribs into individual pieces and serve with barbecue sauce if desired. Enjoy!

Nutrition Values:

Calories: 385; Total Fat: 30g; Saturated Fat: 15g; Protein: 30g; Carbs: 0g; Fiber: 0g Sugar: 0g

VEGAN & VEGETARIAN

80. SMOKED SUMMER VEGETABLES

Preparation Time: 30 minutes
Servings: 4

Ingredients:

- Summer squash
- 2 zucchini
- 1 onion
- 2 cups mushrooms
- 2 cups French-cut green beans

Directions:

1. Wash thoroughly and slice squash, onion, and zucchini, mushrooms, and green beans.
2. Combine all these ingredients and mix well.
3. Preheat the electric smoker to 250°F.
4. Make 4 cup-shaped containers from heavy duty aluminum foil.
5. Put vegetables in these cups.
6. Add herbs and spices to taste.
7. Pinch the top of foil cups together.
8. Make several holes in the foil so that the smoke can circulate around the vegetables. Smoke for 1 hr. at 220°F.

Nutrition Value:
Calories: 97
Protein: 5.6g
Carbs: 14g
Fat: 9g

81. HERBY SMOKED CAULIFLOWER

Preparation Time: 20 minutes
Servings: 4

Ingredients:

- 1 head cauliflower
- Olive oil
- Salt
- Pepper
- 2 tsps. dried oregano
- 2 tsps. Dried basil

Directions:

1. Start by soaking your woodchips for about an hour and preheating your smoker to 200°F/93°C.
2. Remove the woodchips from the liquid then pat dry before using.
3. Then take your cauliflower and chop into medium-sized pieces, removing the core.
4. Place the pieces of cauliflower onto a sheet pan and then drizzle with the olive oil.
5. Sprinkle the seasonings and herbs over the cauliflower then pop into the smoker.
6. Smoke for 2 hours, checking and turning often.
7. Serve and enjoy!

Nutrition Value:

Calories: 31
Protein: 1.5g
Carbs: 6.7g
Fat: 0.34g

82. SMOKED GREEN BEANS WITH LEMON

Preparation Time: 20 minutes
Serving 4

Ingredients

- 2 lbs. fresh green beans, trimmed and soaked
- 2 tbsps. Apple vinaigrette dressing
- 1 lemon

Directions:

1. Place beans in a colander.
2. Preheat smoker to 140°F and add wood chips (recommended Oak wood chips).
3. Place the beans in the pan in a single layer and lightly coat with the dressing.
4. Place the beans on the upper shelf of the smoker and smoke for 1 hour.
5. Remove from the heat, cover with foil and let rest for 15 minutes.
6. Pour lemon juice, sprinkle with the lemon zest and serve.

Nutrition Value:

Calories: 74.31
Total Fat: 0.66g
Total Carbs: 17.02g
Protein: 4.19g

83. SMOKED LEMONY-GARLIC ARTICHOKES

Preparation Time: 20 minutes
Servings: 4

Ingredients:

- 4 artichokes
- 4 minced garlic cloves
- 3 tbsps. Lemon juice
- ½ c. virgin olive oil
- 2 parsley sprigs

- Sea salt

Directions:
1. Put a large pot on your stove with a metal steaming basket inside.
2. Fill with water just to the bottom of the basket and bring to a boil.
3. Cut the artichoke tail and take out the toughest leaves.
4. With cooking shears, clip the pointy ends off of the outermost leaves.
5. Cut the artichokes in half lengthwise. Remove the hairy choke in the center.
6. Put the halves, stem side down, in the steamer basket. Reduce the heat to a rolling simmer.
7. On the pot, cover and steam for about 20 to 25 minutes, until the inside of the artichoke is tender.
8. Prepare a dressing: place in a mortar the garlic, lemon juice, olive oil, parsley, and salt.
9. Take away the basket and let the artichokes come to room temperature.
10. Preheat your smoker to 200°F.
11. Place the artichokes in aluminum foil packets and brush garlic mixture all over the artichokes.
12. Smoke the artichoke halves for approximately 1 hour.
13. Serve hot.

Nutrition Value:
Calories: 83.22
Total Fat: 0.29g
Total Carbs: 18.82g
Protein: 5.54g

84. SMOKED PORTOBELLO MUSHROOMS WITH HERBS DE PROVENCE

Preparation Time: 10 minutes
Servings: 4

Ingredients

- 12 large Portobello mushrooms
- 1 tbsp. Herbs de Provence
- ¼ c. extra virgin olive oil
- Sea salt
- Black pepper

Preparation:

1. Preheat smoker to 200°F and add wood chips (recommended oak wood chips).
2. In a bowl, mix Herbs de Provence, olive oil, salt, and pepper to taste.
3. Clean the mushrooms with a dry cloth or paper towel.
4. Rub the mushrooms all over with herbs mixture.
5. Place the mushrooms, cap side down, directly on the top grill rack. Smoke for approximately 2 hours.
6. Remove carefully so the herbal liquid in the cap remains in place.
7. Serve whole and enjoy!

Nutrition Value:

Calories: 146.08
Fat: 13.63g
Total Carbs: 5.22g
Protein: 3.03g

85. SMOKY CORN ON THE COB

Preparation Time: 10 minutes
Servings: 5

Ingredients:

- 10 ears sweet corn
- ½ c. butter
- Salt
- Black pepper

Directions:

1. Preheat your smoker to 225°F and add wood chips (recommended oak or hickory).

2. Put the ears of corn on the top 2 racks of the smoker and smoke for 2 hours.
3. Rotate the corn every 30 minutes.
4. Serve hot with butter, salt, and pepper.

Nutrition Value:

Calories: 408.72
Total Fat: 22.27g
Total Carbs: 53.5g
Protein: 9.55g

86. SMOKED POTATO SALAD

Preparation Time: 30 mins
Servings: 4

Ingredients:

- 3 eggs, hard-boiled
- 2 tbsps. cider vinegar
- 1 lb. russet potatoes
- 1 tbsp. Dijon mustard
- ½ c. red onion
- ⅓ c. light mayonnaise
- Salt
- Black pepper

Directions:

1. Preheat the electric smoker to 225°F.
2. Put prepared wood chips in the wood tray — use mesquite chips for the best result.
3. Put peeled potatoes in a saucepan and cover with water. Put on the lid and bring to a boil.
4. Cook for 20 mins. Pat potatoes dry, and put them on paper towels.
5. Directly smoke potatoes on the racks for 2 hrs. as you add extra wood chips in a cycle of 45 mins.
6. Remove potatoes, let them cool.
7. Chop them well for the preparation of the salad.
8. Combine boiled eggs, onion, mayonnaise, pickles, mustard,

pepper, salt, and vinegar.
9. Mix all these ingredients well.
10. Add potatoes to the prepared mixture. Put in the fridge for several hrs. covered.

Nutrition Value:
Calories: 209
Total Fat: 9g
Total Carbs: 30g
Protein: 3g

87. SMOKED VOLCANO POTATOES

Preparation Time: 15 minutes.
Servings: 2

Ingredients:

- 2 russet potatoes
- ¾ c. sour cream.
- 1 c. cheddar cheese
- 2 tbsps. green onion
- 8 bacon strips
- 4 tbsps. butter
- 2 tbsps. olive oil
- Salt

Preparation
1. Preheat the electric smoker to 250°F.
2. Wash potatoes, pierce using the fork.
3. Take the oil and salt and rub on the potatoes. Wrap the potatoes in foil and put in the smoker.
4. Smoke potatoes for 3 hrs.
5. Cut off the top of each potato and remove the potato flesh, leaving the shell empty.
6. Fry and crumble the bacon. Combine potato flesh with bacon, butter, sour cream, and cheese in a bowl.
7. Put the prepared filling in the potatoes, add some cheese on the top.
8. Wrap the potato with 2 bacon slices — for securing use

toothpicks.

9. Smoke for another 1 hr.
10. Add green onions with a little sour cream on top (sour cream will give a special flavor to the potato).

Nutrition Value:

Calories: 256
Total Fat: 39.3g
Total Carbs: 31.7g
Protein: 32.1g

88. GROOVY SMOKED ASPARAGUS

Preparation Time: 5 minutes
Serving: 4

Ingredients:

- 1 bunch asparagus
- 2 tbsps. Olive oil
- 1 tsp. chopped garlic
- Kosher salt
- ½ tsp. black pepper

Directions:

1. Prepare the water pan of your smoker accordingly
2. Pre-heat your smoker to 275 degrees Fahrenheit/135 degree Celsius
3. Fill a medium-sized bowl with water and add 3-4 handfuls of woods and allow them to soak
4. Add the asparagus to a grill basket in a single layer
5. Drizzle olive oil on top and sprinkle garlic, pepper, and salt
6. Toss them well
7. Put the basket in your smoker
8. Add a few chips into the loading bay and keep repeating until all of the chips after every 20 minutes
9. Smoke for 60-90 minutes
10. Serve and enjoy!

Nutrition Value:

Calories: 68
Total Fat: 4.1g
Total Carbs: 7.1g
Protein: 2.8g

89. SMOKED SQUASH CASSEROLE

Preparation Time: 40 minutes
Servings 2

Ingredients:

- 2½ lbs. yellow squash
- 2 tbsps. parsley flakes
- 2 eggs, beaten
- 1 medium yellow onion
- 1 sleeve saltine crackers
- 1 package Velveeta cheese
- ½ c. Alouette Sundried Tomato
- Basil cheese spread
- ¼ c. Alouette Garlic and Herb cheese spread
- ¼ c. mayonnaise
- ¾ tsp. hot sauce
- ¼ tsp. Cajun seasoning
- ½ c. butter
- ¼ tsp. salt
- ¼ tsp. black pepper

Directions:

1. Preheat the electric smoker to 250°F.
2. Combine squash and onion in a large saucepan and add water to cover. Boil on medium heat until tender.
3. Drain and to this hot mixture, add Velveeta cheese, Alouette cheese, mayonnaise, parsley flakes, hot sauce, Cajun seasoning, salt, and pepper to taste.
4. Stir all together well.
5. Cool a little, add eggs and stir until mixed.
6. Melt butter in a saucepan.
7. Add crushed crackers to the butter and stir well. Combine ½

cup of butter-cracker mix with the squash mixture. Stir thoroughly.

8. Pour into a disposable aluminum foil pan. Top the squash with remaining butter and crackers. Cover the pan tightly with aluminum foil.
9. Put on the lower rack of the smoker and cook for 1 hr. Put one small handful of prepared wood chips in the wood tray for the best result use hickory.
10. After an hour, remove the foil from the casserole and cook for another 15 mins.

Nutrition Value:
Calories: 190
Total Fat: 8g
Total Carbs: 23g
Protein: 7g

90. SMOKED EGGPLANT

Preparation Time: 20 minutes.
Servings: 4

Ingredients:
- 2 medium eggplant
- Olive oil

Directions:
1. Preheat your smoker to 200°F/93°C and soak your wood chips for an hour.
2. Remove the woodchips from the liquid then pat dry before using.
3. Then carefully peel your eggplant then slice into rounds of around ¼"/1cm thick.
4. Brush each of these rounds with olive oil then place directly into the smoker.
5. Smoke for approximately an hour until soft and tender. Serve and enjoy!

Nutrition Value:
Calories: 85

Protein: 1.6g
Carbs: 9.4g
Fat: 4.6g

91. TWICE PULLED POTATOES

Prep time 30 minutes.
Servings 4

Ingredients:

- 1 lb. pulled pork
- 2 russet potatoes
- 1/3 c. sour cream
- 4 oz. cream cheese
- 1/3 c. cheddar cheese
- Chives
- BBQ sauce, to taste

Directions:

1. Preheat the electric smoker to 225°F. Smoke washed potatoes for 2 hours.
2. Mix potato flesh, cheddar cheese, sour cream, cream cheese, pulled pork and BBQ sauce in a bowl and stir well.
3. Put prepared mixture back into potatoes skins.
4. Smoke for another 40 mins.
5. Season with more BBQ sauce, if desired. Sprinkle some cheddar cheese and chives on the top.

Nutrition Value:

Calories: 285
Protein: 3g
Carbs: 24.1g
Fat: 8.1g

SNACKS

92. SMOKED DESSERT PIZZA

Servings: 4
Preparation Time: 20 mins
Cooking Time: 10 mins.

Ingredients:

- 1 can pizza dough
- Marshmallows
- Your choice candies
- Chocolate syrup
- Graham crackers

Directions:

1. Heat up the smoker to 350°F. Spread out the dough and slice it into eight sections. Add the dough to the smoker grate for about five minutes. Sprinkle the toppings, add the sauce, along with the crumbled crackers. Smoke for about five minutes until everything is melted. Set aside and cool for a few minutes before serving.

Nutrition Value:

Calories: 334 Protein: 12.1g Carbs: 33.6g   Fat: 16.8g

BEEF JERKY

Servings: 4
Preparation Time: 10 mins
Cooking Time: 8 hrs.

Ingredients:

- 2 lb. sirloin
- 1 tbsp. cider vinegar
- 1 c. soy sauce

- 4 tbsp. freshly cracked black pepper
- 1 dash of each:
- Worcestershire sauce
- Hot pepper sauce

Directions:

1. Slice the sirloin into ½-inch slices. Whisk the Worcestershire sauce, pepper sauce, vinegar, pepper, and soy sauce in a large mixing container. Toss in the slices of meat, refrigerate and marinate overnight. Set the cooker on low heat and lightly oil the cooking grate. Lay the strips in a single layer and smoke for 6-8 hours. It's done when the edges look dry with a small amount of moisture in the center of each jerky treat.

Nutrition Value:

Calories: 457 Protein: 51.3g Carbs: 21.4g   Fat: 17.7g

94. VENISON ROLLS

Servings: 8
Preparation Time: 10 mins
Cooking Time: 1 hr. 30 mins.

Ingredients:

- 1 lb. Bacon
- 1 lb. Venison meat, cubed
- 1 onion
- 1 green bell pepper
- 1 pkg. cream cheese
- Mesquite Marinate

Directions:

1. Set the temperature on the cooker to 275-300°F. Prepare the meat in a container with the marinade for a minimum of 24 hours. Slice the peppers and cream cheese along with the cream cheese. Add the ingredients in the middle of the cubed venison, rolling the meat together, and wrap with the bacon. Use toothpicks to ensure the cheese doesn't escape during the smoking process. The internal temperature should

reach 190°F approximately (1 to 1 ½ hours).

Nutrition Value:

Calories: 361Protein: 27.9 g Carbs: 21.1g   Fat: 18.5g

95. HAMBURGER JERKY

Servings: 8
Preparation Time: 10 mins
Cooking Time: 4 hrs.

Ingredients:

- 2 lb. lean ground beef
- 1 tbsp. allspice
- 1 minced garlic clove
- 2 t. grated ginger
- ½ c. soy sauce
- Suggested Wood Chips – Hickory or Mesquite

Directions:

1. Make strips from flattened hamburger – 1 ½-inches wide and 5 inches long with a thickness of about ¼-inch. Add a layer of the strips in a dish to marinate. For the Marinade: Add the ingredients in a small dish, blending well. Shake it over the meat, flip, and shake the other side well. Add the strips to the dish, making sure to coat each slice evenly. Cover the bowl and let them rest for 6-10 hours in the fridge. Shuffle the meat several times for even flavoring. Smoke at 140°F for four hours.

Nutrition Value:

Calories: 256Protein: 31.7 g Carbs: 1.8g Fat: 12.7g

96. SMOKEY PIMENTO CHEESE APPETIZER

Servings: 8
Preparation Time: 5 mins
Cooking Time: 1 hr.

Ingredients:

- 1 container (12.oz.) pimento cheese spread
- 1 lb. kielbasa sausage
- Sliced jalapeno peppers
- Saltine crackers

Directions:

1. Warm up the smoker to 225°F in advance. When ready, just add the sausage for 45 min. to 1 hr. Remove from the smoker. Arrange the crackers – salt-side down – with 1 teaspoon of cheese spread. Slice the smoked sausage into ½-inch segments and add along with a jalapeno slice. Enjoy!

Nutrition Value:

Calories: 271 Protein: 17.5g Carbs: 9.7g Fat: 19.4g

97. SWEET TEA PORK JERKY

Servings: 2
Preparation Time: 5 mins
Cooking Time: 3 hrs.

Ingredients:

- 1 cup sweet tea - divided
- ¼ tsp. garlic
- 1 lb. center-cut pork loin – boneless
- ½ tsp. pepper
- 1 ½ tbsp. soy sauce/tamari
- ¼ tsp. onion
- Pinch of red pepper flakes
- ½ tsp. Salt
- Wood Chip Suggested: Apple soaked in water

Directions:

1. Trim away the silver skin from the pork and slice it thin – ¼-inch pieces. Toss into a re-sealable plastic bag.
2. Combine the marinade fixings in the bag and massage until all is well coated. Place in a container overnight in the fridge (to prevent possible bag leakage).

3. About 30 minutes before ready to prepare, remove and let the mixture become room temperature. Meanwhile, soak the chips and set the temperature to 180°F. on the smoker. Add a half and half combination of tea and water to the side drawer.
4. Remove and pat dry the pork with some paper towels and place on the smoker rack (space between each). Smoke for 1 ½ hours. After that time check the water and chips. Add if needed and smoke until done (60-90 additional min.) Check at 30-minute intervals.
5. Calories: 381 Protein: 51.9g Carbs: 7.5g Fat: 19.4g

98. PORK BELLY BURNT ENDS

Servings: 15
Preparation Time: 10 mins
Cooking Time: 1 hr. 45 mins.

Ingredients:

Sauce:
- 3 tbsp. unsalted butter
- 1 c. barbecue sauce
- 2 tbsp. honey

Pork:
- 5 lb. pork belly – in chunks
- 1 c. dry rub
- 3 tbsp. Extra Virgin Olive Oil
- Suggested Wood Chips: Cherry

Directions:

1. Warm up the smoker ahead of time between 225-250°F. Trim away the fat and slice into 2-inch cubes. Pour the olive oil into a large bowl with the meat. Use the dry rub and arrange on a wire rack or right on the smoker rack.
2. Prepare uncovered for 3 hrs. Remove and place in an aluminum pan. Prepare the sauce and pour over the pork. Cover with some foil and put back on the smoker rack for 90 minutes (200°F internal temp.) Remove the foil and close the cover lid. Smoke 15 additional minutes, remove and serve.

3. Calories: 484 Protein: 38.2g Carbs: 13.9g Fat: 29.6g

99. PORK TENDERLOIN APPETIZERS

Servings: 4
Preparation Time: 10 mins
Cooking Time: 2 hrs.

Ingredients:

- 1 (1 ½ lb.) pork tenderloin
- Freshly cracked black pepper
- Sea salt to taste
- Garlic salt
- Pimento cheese dip
- Bruschetta toast
- 1 jar mild jalapeno peppers
- Wood Choice: Hickory

Directions:

1. Warm up the smoker ahead of time to 225°F. and add the chips. Combine the garlic salt, sea salt, and black pepper to season the tenderloin. Arrange in a pan —unwrapped— and smoke 1 to 1 ½ hours (150°F. internal temp.) Remove and wrap with heavy-duty foil. Place back in the cooker for another 30 minutes (165°F internally). When it's done, just slice into ¼ to 3/8-inch medallions and slice into halves. Arrange on Platter. Place the toast, cheese dip, and pepper to serve and enjoy.

Nutrition Value:

Calories: 183Protein: 32.9g Carbs: 1.1g Fat: 4.4g

100. TERIYAKI SMOKED VENISON JERKY

Servings: 6
Preparation Time: 15 mins
Cooking Time: 6 hrs.

Ingredients:

- 1 lb. venison loin or roast
- ¼ c. dry – red wine
- 1/3 cup honey
- 1/3 cup soy sauce
- 1 tbsp. rice wine vinegar – mirin
- 1 tsp. minced ginger
- 1 minced garlic clove
- ½ tsp. salt
- ½ tsp. pepper
- Unsweetened apple juice
- Wood Chip Suggestion: Soaked apple or cherry

Directions:
1. Warm up the smoker to 165°F and fill the water tray with a concentration of ½ water and ½ juice and add the soaked chips. Toss all of the marinade fixings in a sealable plastic baggie or large baking dish. Prepare the venison by slicing 1-inch wide x ¼-inch wide strips and lay them against the grain. Pound each piece several times and add to the bag. Place in the fridge for up to 12 hours.
2. Discard the marinade and pat dry the meat with paper towels. Add to the smoker racks and smoke for 4-6 hours. After 2 ½ hrs., replenish the water and wood chips. When done, let cook, serve, and enjoy!

Nutrition Value:
Calories: 232Protein: 23.2g Carbs: 19.7g   Fat: 7g

101. STOUT BEEF JERKY

Servings: 1
Preparation Time: 1 hr
Cooking Time: 3 hrs. 30 min.

Ingredients:

- London broil- 1 lb., trimmed, cut into strips
- Sea salt- 2 tablespoons
- Apple cider vinegar- ¾ cup, unfiltered

- Blackstrap molasses- 2 tablespoons
- Brown sugar- 2 tablespoons
- Black pepper- 1 tablespoon
- Onion powder- 1 teaspoon
- Garlic powder- 1 teaspoon
- Stout- 1 bottle
- Hickory wood chips
- Mesquite wood chips- soaked in water

Directions:

1. Refrigerate the London broil for about 30 minutes before using. Prepare the marinade by combining all the ingredients and spices. Make sure to mix well. Slice the beef into strips of 1/4" thickness. Place these strips in a baking dish and add the marinade over it. Arrange the strips in a way so that they are marinated properly on each side for best flavors.
2. Cover the dish with a sheet and refrigerate the marinated beef for next 4-8 hours or for overnight. You can also use a re-sealable plastic bag in place of dish and sheet. Remove the beef strips from the dish and discard the excess marinade. Pat the strips dry using paper towels.
3. Layer the beef strips in the smoker and make sure that there is a little space for air left between each strip. Fill the water pan with a mixture of beer or stout and water in 1:1 ratio. Add the soaked mesquite or hickory wood chips to the side or bottom tray. Close the door.
4. Smoke the beef for next 3.5 hours at 180 degrees Fahrenheit. Keep a regular check over the smoke and add more wood chips if required. Once done, take out the jerky and allow it to cool down. Wait for about 10-15 minutes before serving. Serve immediately or store in the refrigerator for further use.

Nutrition Value:
Calories: 240Protein: 50g, Carbs: 1g, Fat: 4g

102. SUMMER SAUSAGE

Servings: 15
Preparation Time: 10 mins

Cooking Time: 9 hrs.

Ingredients:

- 5 tsp. Morton tender quick
- 2 tsp. Crushed red peppers
- 2 tbsp. Morton sugar cure
- 2 tsp. Peppercorns
- 1 tsp. garlic powder
- 2 tsp. Mustard seeds
- 5 lbs. lean hamburger
- 2 tsp. Liquid smoke
- 2 tsp. Coarse pepper

Directions:

1. Add all of the fixings into a Ziploc-type bag and put them in the fridge for three days. Squeeze the bag twice daily. When the meat is ready, set the smoker temperature to 225°F. Make into two-inch diameter rolls and arrange in the cooker. Smoke for approximately 8-9 hours (reach the internal temperature of 160°F).

Nutrition Value:

Calories: 375Protein: 16.1g, Carbs: 50.7g, Fat: 12.1g

103. JALAPENO POPPERS

Servings: 4
Preparation Time: 10 mins
Cooking Time: 1 hr.

Ingredients:

- 8 oz. onion & chive cream cheese
- 12 jalapenos – split and canoed
- 4 oz. sour cream
- ½ c. shredded cheddar & Colby cheese
- Pinch of kosher salt
- Black pepper
- Thin bacon

- Garlic powder
- Chosen Wood Chips: Hickory

Directions:

1. Combine all of the fixings (omit the bacon and jalapenos for now). And place in a freezer bag. Split and remove the seeds from the jalapenos. Spread or pipe (cut a hole in the corner of the bag) the filling into the peppers and cover with a slice of bacon. Secure with toothpicks. Smoke one hour at 275°F.

Nutrition Value:

Calories: 286Protein: 9.5g, Carbs: 7.3g, Fat: 24.8g

104. TRI-TIP ROAST AND HORSERADISH CHEVRE CROSTINI

Servings: 4
Preparation Time: 10 mins
Cooking Time: 30 mins.

Ingredients:

- 3 pack of tri-tip roasts
- Chevre goat cheese
- Coarse and fine black pepper
- Olive oil
- Fresh horseradish – not creamed
- 2 baguettes

Directions:

2. The evening before, rub down the roasts with the fine and coarse black pepper. Use plenty of horseradish as well. When ready to prepare, set the smoker to 225°F. Add two of the roasts on the bottom and one on the top. Slice the baguettes into 1/3-inch slices and arrange them in a bowl. Toss with the oil for an even coating. Spread out the bread on a baking pan and quick broil to toast. Spread the Chevre on the toast.

3. When the meat reaches 125°F, it is medium rare. Let it cool for 15 minutes. Slice up the first roast thinly and save the others as needed. Prepare the sandwich with the desired

fixings and enjoy.

Nutrition Value:
Calories: 318Protein: 43.3g, Carbs: 1.1g, Fat: 14.4g

105. CANDIED BACON

Servings: 10
Preparation Time: 5 mins
Cooking Time: 1 hr. 30 mins.

Ingredients:
- ¼ cup brown sugar
- ¼ cup maple syrup
- 1 lb. thick-sliced bacon

Directions:
1. Remove the racks from the smoker and set the temperature for 210°F. Prepare the bacon on a cookie sheet or waxed paper. Drizzle with the syrup and spread with a pastry brush. Sprinkle with the sugar and arrange on the smoker racks. Smoke for 1 ½ hrs. Serve as a salty snack or alongside some eggs.

Nutrition Value:
Calories: 226Protein: 5.7g, Carbs: 11.1g, Fat: 17.8g

106. CHEX MIX

Servings: 8
Preparation Time: 15 mins
Cooking Time: 1 hr. 30 mins.

Ingredients:
- Chex cereal, 3 cups, wheat
- ½ tsp. onion powder
- Chex cereal, 3 cups, rice
- ¾ tsp. garlic powder
- Chex cereal, 3 cups, corn

- Pretzels, 1 cup, bite-sized
- 3 tbsp. Worcestershire sauce
- 6 tbsp. butter
- 1 tsp. cayenne
- 1 cup mixed nuts
- 1 cup mixed nuts
- 1½ tsp. seasoned salt
- Wood Suggested: Apple chips

Directions:

1. Warm up the smoker until it reaches 250°F. Add the wood chips. In a small pan, melt the butter and combine with the season salt, Worcestershire sauce, onion powder, cayenne pepper, and garlic powder.
2. Toss the nuts, cereal, and pretzels together in a disposable pan. Pour the hot mixture over the dry fixings and mix well. Smoke for 1 – 1 ½ hours (stir every 15 min.) Let it cool before serving.

Nutrition Value:

Calories: 416Protein: 6.4g, Carbs: 51.9g, Fat: 22.7g

107. BACON WRAPS

Servings: 20
Preparation Time: 5 mins
Cooking Time: 2 hr. 30 mins.

Ingredients:

- 1 pkg. (16 oz.) cocktail sausages
- 1 lb. pkg. bacon
- 13 c. packed brown sugar
- Wood Suggestion: Hickory

Directions:

1. Set the temperature of the smoker at 275°F. Slice the bacon lengthwise into 1/3 segments. Wrap each piece around the sausage. Roll each one in the brown sugar and secure with a toothpick. Arrange on a baking tin. Place on the rack and

smoke 2 to 2 ½ hours until crispy.

Nutrition Value:

Calories: 672Protein: 6.8g, Carbs: 143.9g, Fat: 10.8g

108. NUTTY CHOCOLATE BANANAS

Servings: 2-4
Preparation Time: 10 mins
Cooking Time: 1 hrs. 30 mins.

Ingredients:

- 4 small bananas, semi-ripe
- ½ tsp. sea salt
- 2-3 Tbsp. dark chocolate, chopped fine
- 4-6 tsp. hazelnuts, chopped, toasted
- Vanilla ice cream, to serve

Directions:

1. Preheat your smoker to 250°F/120°C and soak your wood chips for an hour. Remove the wood chips from the liquid then pat dry before using. Peel the banana in half so that the top part of the banana is exposed but the bottom is still sitting in its skin. Make a few slits in the banana then place into your smoker for 5 minutes. Remove the bananas from the smoker then sprinkle with salt, chocolate and topped nuts. Serve with a generous scoop of ice-cream and enjoy.

Nutrition Value:

Calories: 241 Protein: 3.8g, Carbs: 39.8g, Fat: 9.3g

109. PLUM PIE

Servings: 6
Preparation Time: 10 mins
Cooking Time: 40 mins.

Ingredients:

- 4-5 plums, thinly sliced

- 1/4 cup (50g) sugar
- 1 Tbsp. cornstarch
- Flour
- 1 refrigerated pie crust, softened as directed on box
- 1/4 cup (80g) peach preserve

Directions:

1. Preheat your smoker to 275 and soak your wood chips for an hour. Remove the wood chips from the liquid then pat dry before using. Then take a medium bowl and add the plums, sugar, and cornstarch then stir well until combined. Pop to one side. Now dust your work surface with flour and roll out the pie crust.
2. Place the pie crust into a pie pan without greasing it first. Spread the preserve into the bottom of the pie, then top with plum slices. Pop into the smoker and cook for 30-40 minutes until bubbly and brown. Remove from the smoker, let it rest for 10 minutes then serve and enjoy!

Nutrition Value:

Calories: 236 Protein: 2.2g, Carbs: 39.8g, Fat:8.4g

110. UPSIDE DOWN CAKE

Servings: 8
Preparation Time: 20 mins
Cooking Time: 45 mins.

Ingredients:

- Cake
- 1 Tbsp. unsalted butter, for greasing
- ¼ tsp. salt
- 9 tbsp unsalted butter, room temperature
- 3 free-range eggs
- 1 tsp. vanilla
- 1 ½ cups (190g) cake flour, sifted
- ¾ tsp. baking powder

- ¾ cup (150g) granulated sugar
- ¼ tsp. baking soda
- 8 Tbsp. sour cream
- For the fruit and glaze…
- 1 pineapple, peeled, cored, cut into rings
- 4 cherries, cut in half
- 4 Tbsp. unsalted butter, room temperature
- ½ cup (100g) brown sugar

Directions:
1. Preheat your smoker to 250°F and soak your wood chips for an hour. Remove the wood chips from the liquid then pat dry before using. Next grab a 10" (25cm) cake pan and grease well with butter. Take a medium bowl and cream the butter and sugar together.
2. Place the fruit into the bottom of the cake pan, then put the sugar and butter mixture (from the fruit and glaze ingredients) over the top. Pop to one side. Next take another bowl and add sugar and butter, then beat until fluffy and light.
3. Add vanilla and eggs then beat for another minute. Lastly, add the salt, baking powder, sour cream and flour then stir well to combine. Pour this cake batter over the fruit then pop into the smoker. Cook for 35-45 minutes until cooked through. Remove from the smoker, rest for 10 minutes then serve and enjoy.

Nutrition Value:
Calories: 385 Protein: 6.8g, Carbs: 48.2g, Fat: 18.6g

111. BELGIAN BEER BROWNIES

Servings: 15
Preparation Time: 20 mins
Cooking Time: 1 hr.

Ingredients:
- 2 cups Three Philosophers ale
- 2 cups unbleached all-purpose white flour

- 10 ounces chocolate, unsweetened
- 4 cups granulated sugar
- 1/8 teaspoon salt
- Confectioner's sugar, for dusting (optional)
- 4 ounces bittersweet eating chocolate, chopped into ½ inch pieces
- 2 cups butter, unsalted
- 8 large eggs
- 2 teaspoons pure vanilla extract

Directions:

1. Pour ale into a heavy bottomed saucepan. Place the saucepan over high heat. Bring to the boil. Continue boiling until it reduces to half its original quantity. Transfer into a heatproof dish. Toss bittersweet chocolate and 2 tablespoons flour in a bowl and set aside. Wipe the saucepan clean and place it back on low heat. Add butter. When the butter melts, use a little of it and grease a large baking dish. Place the dish in the refrigerator for 5-6 minutes. Remove the dish from the refrigerator and sprinkle 1-2 tablespoons flour all over the buttered area.

2. Add unsweetened chocolate to the saucepan and melt the chocolate stirring constantly. Remove from heat. Whisk together eggs and granulated sugar in a bowl. Add the ale or stout and whisk again. Add vanilla, salt and melted chocolate and whisk again. Add remaining flour and fold gently. Add chocolate chunks and fold again. Pour the batter into the prepared baking dish. Alternately, you can pour into a cast iron skillet. Preheat the smoker to 275°F following the manufacturer's instructions. Place the baking dish in the smoker and smoke for about 40 minutes or a toothpick when inserted in the center comes out clean. Remove from the smoker and cool completely. Cut into 24 squares and serve.

Nutrition Value:
Calories: 486 Protein: 4.1g, Carbs: 54.7g, Fat: 27.4g

112. BAKED LEMON MERINGUE PIE

Servings: 6-8
Preparation Time: 20 mins
Cooking Time: 30 mins.

Ingredients:

For filling:

- 1 ½ cups (300g) sugar
- 2/3 cup (160ml) lemon juice
- 1 Tbsp. lemon zest
- Pinch of salt
- 4 Tbsp. unsalted butter
- 3 free range eggs + 3 egg yolks

For Pie:

- 1 pie dough
- 1 Tbsp. heavy cream
- 1 free range egg
- For meringue:
- Eggs (3, whites only)
- 4-5 Tbsp. sugar
- Vanilla extract (1 tsp.)

Directions:

1. Preheat your smoker to 250°F/120°C and soak your wood chips for an hour. Remove the wood chips from the liquid then pat dry before using. Take a medium bowl and add the sugar, lemon juice, lemon zest and salt. Stir well to combine. Next pour this mixture onto a greased baking sheet then place into your smoker for 30 minutes. Remove from the smoker and set to one side.
2. Turn up the temperature of your smoker 275°F and grease your pie dish. Sprinkle your work surface with flour and start to roll out the pie dough until it's approximately 1/8" (1/4 cm). Place into the pie dish then push down well. Pop into the freezer for 30 minutes. Meanwhile, take a small bowl and add the cream and one of the eggs. Stir well to combine then brush over the edges of the pie.
3. Transfer the pie to the smoker and cook for 10 minutes. Remove and allow it to cool. Now let's make the filling. Take

116

a large bowl and add 3 eggs and 3 egg yolks (keep hold of whites), whisk, and stir in the lemon mixture. Mix well. Using a Bain Marie or double boiler, warm the lemon mixture for 10 minutes until it thickens nicely. Keep stirring.

4. Remove this filling from the heat and whisk in the butter. Pour the lemon mixture into the pie crust and place back into the smoker for 20 minutes until the filling has set. Cool overnight in the fridge. Add the egg whites and sugar to a bowl then place in a Bain Marie or double boiler to warm through. Keep stirring until the sugar has dissolved.

5. Remove from the heat then beat with a whisk the egg whites until they are white and fluffy. Add the vanilla then beat again. Pipe the meringue onto the top of the pie then use a kitchen torch to brown the top. Serve and enjoy!

Nutrition Value:

Calories: 307 Protein: 4.7g, Carbs: 39.8g, Fat: 14.6g

113. SMOKED PLUMS

Servings: 3-6
Preparation Time: 10 mins
Cooking Time: 30 mins.

Ingredients:

- 6 fresh plums, cut in half and stones removed (or as many as you can fit into your smoker)
- 1 cup (90g) wood chips of your choice

Directions:

1. Preheat your smoker to 200°F/93°C and soak the wood chips for an hour. Remove the wood chips from the liquid then pat dry before using. Place the plums directly into your smoker and cook for 30 minutes – the first 20 with the skin down, the final 10 with the skin up. Remove from the smoker, and serve warm with meats, in salads or even as a special way to round off your meal. Enjoy!

Nutrition Value:

Calories: 117 Protein: 2.7g, Carbs: 28.6g, Fat: 0.8g

114. SMOKED PEACH CRUMBLE

Servings: 15
Preparation Time: 10 mins
Cooking Time: 1 hr.

Ingredients:
For the pie filling:
- 3 teaspoons all-purpose flour
- 1 teaspoon ground cinnamon
- 1 cup sugar
- 3 pounds peaches, peeled, cored, sliced into ¼ inch wedges

For crumble:
- 2 cups rolled oats
- ½ teaspoon baking powder
- ½ teaspoon baking soda
- 1 cup butter, melted
- 2 cups brown sugar
- Ice cream to serve

Directions:
1. Preheat the smoker to 275°F following the manufacturer's instructions. Make the pie filling as follows: Mix together in a bowl all the pie-filling ingredients and toss well. Transfer into 14-15 ramekins (2/3 fill it). Do not grease the ramekins.
2. To make crumble: Mix together in a bowl flour, brown sugar, oats, baking powder and baking soda. Pour butter over it and mix well. Place about ¼ cup of this mixture over each of the ramekins (over the peach filling). Place the ramekins on the center rack in the smoker and smoke for an hour. Remove the ramekins from the smoker and invert onto individual serving bowls. Serve as it is or with a scoop of ice cream.

Nutrition Value:
Calories: 267 Protein: 2.6g, Carbs: 41.4g, Fat: 13.3g

115. SMOKE ROASTED APPLE CRISP

Servings: 12
Preparation Time: 15 mins
Cooking Time: 1 hr.

Ingredients:

- 12 sweet apples, peeled, cored, cut into 1/8 pieces each
- 3 tablespoons fresh lemon juice
- 3 tablespoons arrowroot or cornstarch
- 12 tablespoons cold butter, chopped into pieces
- ¾ teaspoon lemon zest, grated
- 1 2/3 cups sugar or to taste
- 1/8 teaspoon salt
- 3 teaspoons ground cinnamon
- ¾ cup granola
- ¾ cup flour
- ¾ cup brown sugar, firmly packed
- Apple ice cream of cinnamon ice cream to serve (optional)

Directions:

1. Place apples in a glass bowl. Add lemon juice and lemon zest and toss well. Add 2/3-cup sugar, 2 teaspoons ground cinnamon and arrowroot and toss well. Taste and adjust the sugar if required. Transfer into a cast iron skillet and set aside. Add rest of the ingredients except ice cream into the food processor bowl and pulse until the mixture is coarse in texture. Do not pulse for long. Sprinkle this mixture over the apples in the skillet. Preheat the smoker to 275°F following the manufacturer's instructions. Place the cast iron skillet in the smoker. Smoke until the mixture is crisp and golden brown on top. It should take 45-60 minutes. Remove from the smoker and cool for a while. Serve warm as it is or with ice cream.

Nutrition Value:

Calories: 341 Protein: 1.5g, Carbs: 61.1g, Fat: 11.9g

116. TANGERINE SMOKED FLANS

Servings: 10
Preparation Time: 15 mins
Cooking Time: 1 hr. 30 mins.

Ingredients:

For caramel:
- ½ cup water
- 2 cups sugar

For flan:
- 1 cup sugar
- 4 large egg yolks
- 6 large eggs
- 1/8 teaspoon salt
- 2 cups half and half
- 2 regular or smoked vanilla bean, split, scrape the seeds or 2 teaspoons pure vanilla extract
- 2 sticks cinnamon
- 2 ½ cups whole milk
- 12 strips tangerine zest

Directions:

2. To make caramel: Place a heavy saucepan over high heat. Add sugar and water and stir. Cover and cook for 2 minutes. Lower heat to medium and uncover. Cook until the sugar caramelizes and is golden brown in color. Do not stir during this process. Remove from heat and pour into 10-12 ramekins. Wear kitchen gloves and swirl the ramekins so that the caramelized sugar coats the bottom as well as the sides. Set aside the ramekins to cool. It will harden. Place the ramekins on a rimmed baking sheet.
3. Meanwhile make the flan as follows: Add eggs, yolks, sugar and salt in a large heatproof bowl and whisk until well combined. Place a heavy saucepan over medium heat. Add milk, half and half, tangerine zest, cinnamon and vanilla bean. Heat for a few minutes until warm. Remove from heat.
4. Add about ½ cup of this mixture into the bowl of eggs and whisk. Continue this process until all the milk mixture is added to the egg mixture, whisking each time. Add vanilla

essence if using and whisk again. Cool for a while. Pour into the ramekins. Preheat the smoker to 250°F following the manufacturer's instructions. Place the baking sheet with ramekin cups in the smoker. Smoke for around 1 ½ hours or until the flan is set. Remove from the smoker and cool completely. Chill for 5-6 hours in the refrigerator.

5. To serve: Run a knife around the edges of the flan. Invert onto a plate and serve.

Nutrition Value:

Calories: 315 Protein: 6.3g, Carbs: 49g, Fat: 10.5g

117. ROASTED PEARS

Servings: 8
Preparation Time: 15 mins
Cooking Time: 1 hr.

Ingredients:

- 8 large pears, halved lengthwise, cored
- ½ teaspoon nutmeg, grated
- 10 tablespoons butter, at room temperature
- 1 teaspoon ground cinnamon
- 10 tablespoons ground hazelnuts
- 1 teaspoon ground cloves
- 2 teaspoons vanilla extract
- Juice of a lemon
- 2 cups Poire Williams (Pear Brandy)
- 10 tablespoons brown sugar
- 1 teaspoon lemon zest, grated
- 2 tablespoons rum

Directions:

1. Brush cut part of the pear with lemon juice. Add sugar and butter into a bowl and beat until fluffy. Add vanilla, lemon zest, cloves, graham cracker crumbs, nutmeg, and cinnamon then beat until well combined. Fill this mixture in the pears in the cavity of the core.

2. Place the stuffed apples in a greased disposable aluminum foil pan. Preheat the smoker to 275°F following the manufacturer's instructions. Place the disposable pan in the smoker. Smoke until the apples are soft. It should take 45-60 minutes. But keep a check. Remove from the smoker.

3. Remove the pears from the disposable pan and place on a fireproof platter. Pour Poire Williams in a saucepan and place the saucepan over medium heat. Warm it and remove from heat. Light a matchstick and touch it to the brandy. It will catch fire. Pour the brandy along with the flame on the pears and serve.

Nutrition Value:
Calories: 420 Protein: 2.2g, Carbs: 54.9g, Fat: 16.8g

118. WHITE CHOCOLATE BREAD PUDDING

Servings: 15
Preparation Time: 20 mins
Cooking Time: 1 hr. 30 mins

Ingredients:
- 2 pounds brioche, cubed
- 4 cups whole milk
- 1/8 teaspoon salt
- 16 ounces white chocolate, coarsely chopped
- 4 large egg yolks
- 8 large eggs
- 2 teaspoons pure vanilla extract (use 4 teaspoons extract if not using vanilla beans)
- 2 vanilla beans (optional), halved, scrape the seeds
- 6 cups heavy whipping cream
- Butter for greasing
- 3 cups sugar
- Smoked ice cream to serve

Directions:
1. Preheat the smoker to 250°F following the manufacturer's

instructions. Take a large disposable aluminum foil and place the bread cubes in it in a single layer. Place the pan in the smoker and smoke for 30-45 minutes until the bread cubes are toasted.

2. Meanwhile, add eggs, yolks, vanilla extract and salt in a large heatproof bowl and whisk until well combined. Place a heavy saucepan over medium heat. Add milk, cream, sugar and vanilla bean as well as its seeds. Heat for a few minutes until hot and the sugar is dissolved. Remove from heat.

3. Add half the chocolate and stir constantly until it melts. Cool for a while. Add about ½ cup of this mixture into the bowl of eggs and whisk constantly. Continue this process until all the milk mixture is added to the egg mixture, whisking each time. Add vanilla essence if using and whisk again. Add the toasted bread cubes into it and stir.

4. Grease a cast iron skillet with butter. Pour the entire mixture into the skillet. Sprinkle remaining chocolate pieces on it. Preheat the smoker to 275°F following the manufacturer's instructions. Place the skillet in the smoker. Smoke for around 45 minutes to 1-½ hours (depending on what temperature you have set the smoker) or until set. Remove from the smoker and serve hot with smoked ice cream.

Nutrition Value:
Calories: 780 Protein: 14.6g, Carbs: 67.6g Fat: 50.5g

SIDES

119. SMOKED VEGETABLES

Servings: 6
Preparation Time: 15 minutes

Ingredients:

- 1 ear of fresh corn, husks and silks removed
- 1 medium yellow squash, cut into ½ inch thick slices

- 1 small red onion, cut into thin wedges
- 1 small green pepper, cunt into 1 inch strips
- 1 small red pepper, cut into 1 inch strips
- 1 cup mushrooms, halved
- 2 tbsp. vegetable oil
- 2 tbsp. chicken seasoning
- Smoke Time: 18 Mins
- Smoke Temp: 250

Directions:

1. In a large bowl toss the vegetables with some oil. Sprinkle the chicken seasoning over them. Place all the vegetables in a grill basket.
2. Place vegetables in the smoker. Be sure to turn them every few minutes.
3. Once done the vegetables will be tender. Serve while still warm.

120. FOUR CHEESE SMOKED MAC 'N' CHEESE

This creamy mac 'n' cheese is melt in your mouth delicious. It's savory, and combines four cheeses to give you that childhood favorite everyone grew up with. Sprinkle some bacon bits on the top for extra bit of flavor to make this a real treat.

Servings: 4

Preparation Time: 15 minutes

Ingredients:

- (16-ounce) package elbow macaroni
- 1/4 cup butter
- 1/4 cup all-purpose flour
- 3 cups milk
- 1 (8-ounce) package cream cheese, cut into large chunks
- 1 tbsp. salt
- 1/2 tbsp. black pepper
- 2 cups (8 ounces) extra sharp Cheddar cheese, shredded

- 2 cups (8 ounces) Gouda cheese, shredded
- 1 cup (4 ounces) Parmesan cheese, shredded
- Smoke Time: 1 Hour
- Smoke Temp: 225

Directions:

1. Be sure to cook the pasta first according to the directions. Get a medium saucepan, melt the butter, and then be sure to whisk the flour with the butter. Allow it to cook over a medium heat for only two minutes. Whisk in the milk. Bring it all to a boil for five minutes. Add in the cream cheese, stirring until the entire mixture has become smooth. Next, add in the pepper and salt.
2. Get a large bowl. Mix together cream sauce, 1 cup cheddar, 1 cup gouda cheese, pasta, and parmesan cheese. Transfer the mixture to an aluminum roasting pan. Sprinkle all the leftover gouda and cheddar cheese on top of the mixture.
3. Place the mac 'n' cheese in the smoker.
4. It should turn brown and be bubbly once done. Serve while still warm.

121. BACON-WRAPPED CHEESY STUFFED JALAPENOS

Servings: 4
Preparation Time: 15 minutes

Ingredients:

- 12 fresh jalapeño peppers
- 8 ounces cream cheese, softened to room temperature
- 1 cup shredded cheddar cheese
- 1 clove garlic, chopped
- 1/2 tbsp. smoked paprika
- 12 slices bacon, cut in half
- Smoke Time: 60 Mins
- Smoke Temp: 275

Directions:

1. Cut each of the jalapeno peppers lengthwise. Take out the center membrane and seeds.
2. Combine the paprika, cream cheese, garlic, and cheddar cheese together. Add salt for taste. Spoon this mixture into the cut peppers.
3. Wrap each of the jalapeno peppers in a half slice of bacon. Stick a toothpick through each one to keep them in place.
4. Place the jalapenos in the smoker
5. Serve immediately after they're done smoking.

122. WICKED BAKED BEANS

Servings: 24
Preparation Time: 15 minutes

Ingredients:
- 1/2 lb bacon (cut into 1/2-inch squares)
- 1/2 medium onion, diced
- 1/2green bell pepper, diced
- 1 -2 jalapeno, diced (seeding is optional depending on desired heat)
- 1 (55 ounce) canbush's original baked beans or 1 (55 ounce) canbush's maple baked beans
- 8 ounces canned crushed pineapple, drained
- 1 cup dark brown sugar, firmly packed
- 1 cup ketchup
- 1/2 tbsp. ground dry mustard
- Smoke Time: 2 ½ Hours
- Smoke Temp: 250

Directions:
1. In a skillet be sure to cook the bacon until it's crisp or smoke it.
2. Sauté the onion, bell pepper, and jalapeno until tender.
3. Be sure to combine all ingredients.
4. In a baking pan pour all the ingredients into it.
5. Place the beans in the smoker.
6. When the beans are ready either serve right away, or cover

up and save for later.

123. SMOKED TROUT POTATO SKINS

Servings: 4
Preparation Time: 15 minutes

Ingredients:

- 8 (3-inch-long) russet potatoes (about 2 1/4 lb.s), scrubbed and thoroughly dried
- 2 tsp. unsalted butter (1/4 stick), melted
- Kosher salt
- Freshly ground black pepper
- 1 tbsp. grapeseed or vegetable oil
- 1/2 tbsp. lime juice
- 2 cups baby arugula, washed and dried
- 1 cup Smoked Trout Pâté
- Smoke Time: 2 Hours, 5 Mins
- Smoke Temp: 275°

Directions:

1. Be sure to pierce each potato with a fork. Place on the rack in the smoker, and allow them to smoke for two hours. Once they're done, place they on a wire rack. Allow them to cool for ten minutes so you can handle them.
2. Cut each potato lengthwise. Scoop out all the flesh of the potato, leaving only ¼ inch of the meat inside intact. Coat the insides of the potato with melted butter, pepper, and salt. Do the same for the skin of the potato on both sides.
3. Place potatoes back in the smoker, and allow them to smoke for about six to ten minutes.
4. In a medium bowl mix together lime juice and oil. Add in the arugula at this point. Mix it with the mixture. Divide this mixture among the skins. Top each one off with a tbsp. of the trout pate. Place back in the smoker, and smoke for an additional 5 minutes. Serve afterwards.

124. SMOKED POTATO SALAD

Servings: 4
Preparation Time: 15 minutes

Ingredients:

- 1/4 cup olive oil, divided
- 1/2 tbsp. black pepper
- 1/4 tbsp. kosher salt
- 1 1/2 lb.s small potatoes
- 1/3 cup sliced pitted kalamata olives
- 2 thinly sliced green onions
- 2 tsp. chopped fresh flat-leaf parsley
- 1 tbsp. red wine vinegar
- 2 tsp. celery seed
- 1 tbsp. Dijon mustard
- Smoke Time: 35 Mins
- Smoke Temp: 275

Directions:

1. Mix together potatoes, 1 tbsp. oil, salt, and pepper in a medium bowl. Toss everything to coat them.
2. Arrange all the potatoes on a foil pan in one layer. Close the lid of the smoker once you put the potatoes in there.
3. Once done, take the potatoes out and transfer them to a medium bowl. Mix together the onions and olives in the bowl with the potatoes.
4. Add in the parsley, oil, and the last of the ingredients into a small bowl. Stir it altogether with a whisk. Sprinkle this mixture over the potatoes. Toss to get them coated evenly, and serve.

125. SMOKED SALMON DEVILED EGGS

Servings: 4
Preparation Time: 20 minutes

Ingredients:

- 8 extra-large eggs
- 1/2 cup sour cream

- 2 ounces cream cheese, at room temperature
- 2 tsp. good mayonnaise
- 1 tbsp. freshly squeezed lemon juice
- 2 tsp. minced fresh chives, plus extra for garnish
- 4 ounces good smoked salmon, minced
- 1 tbsp. kosher salt
- 1/2 tbsp. freshly ground black pepper
- 2 ounces salmon roe
- Smoke Time: 4 Mins
- Smoke Temp: 225

Directions:

1. In a large pot, bring water to a boil. Place the eggs in the pot, cover it up, and allow them to boil for 15 minutes. Drain the water from the pot and fill it again with cold water. Allow the eggs to cool.
2. Peel the shell off the eggs. Cut them in half, lengthwise only. Scoop the yolks out carefully with a spoon. Put the bowl of a electric mixer. Place the eggs whites on a platter and set them aside. Sprinkle them with a little bit of salt as well.
3. Add pepper, sour cream, salt, cream cheese, salmon, mayonnaise, chives, and lemon juice to the egg yolks. Beat them at a medium speed in the mixer so everything becomes fluffy. Use a small spoon to fill the eggs whites back up with the mixed egg yolk.
4. Cover the eggs loosely with plastic wrap, and then store them in the fridge for half an hour.
5. Add a dollop of salmon roe on top of the eggs.
6. Place the eggs on the smoker rack. Afterwards, sprinkle them with some pepper and salt before serving.

126. SMOKED CABBAGE

Servings: 2
Preparation Time: 10 minutes

Ingredients:

- 1 Whole cabbage

- butter
- 2-3 chicken or beef bouillon cubes
- Smoke Time: 5 Hours
- Smoke Temp: 225

Directions:
1. In the cavity of the cabbage, cut out a hole that is two to three inches big.
2. In the cavity, pack it with butter and bouillon cubes.
3. Use heavy duty foil to wrap up the cabbage, but not the top.
4. Place cabbage in smoker. Add more butter when needed.
5. Eat the cabbage once it's done.

127. SMOKY OKRA

Servings: 4
Preparation Time: 5 minutes

Ingredients:
- 1 lb. Okra
- Smoked Paprika
- 1tbsp. vegetable oil
- ¾ tsp. salt
- Smoke Time: 10 Mins
- Smoke Temp: 225

Directions:
1. Place the okra in a large bowl, and toss it with the oil, salt, and paprika.
2. Put the okra on wooden skewers.
3. Place the okra on the smoker. Turn the okra over halfway through smoking.
4. Once done eat it while it's still warm.

128. NAAN

Servings: 6
Preparation Time: 10 minutes

Ingredients:

- 1 (.25 ounce) package active dry yeast
- 1 cup warm water
- 1/4 cup white sugar
- 3 tsp. milk
- 1 egg, beaten
- 2 tsp. salt
- 4 1/2 cups bread flour
- 2 tsp. minced garlic (optional)
- 1/4 cup butter, melted
- Smoke Time: 6 Mins
- Smoke Temp: 250

Directions:

1. Get a large bowl, and dissolve the yeast in some warm water. Leave it to stand for ten minutes. Add in the flour, sugar, salt, egg, and milk. This will make the dough. Knead it for eight minutes on a surface that has been lightly floured.
2. Now place the dough in a boil that was rubbed with oil. Cover the top with a damp cloth, and place it aside. Allow the dough to rise for one hour.
3. Punch down on your dough. Knead in the garlic. Begin to pinch off handfuls of the dough. Roll them to the size of golf balls, and put on a tray. Cover them up with a towel, and allow them to rise for half an hour.
4. Once the dough is done rising place the dough in the smoker. It should be browned lightly. Brush the uncooked side with some butter. Turn the dough over halfway through.
5. Repeat step 4 until all the Naan is smoked.

129. SMOKED ZUCCHINI

Servings: 1
Preparation Time: 5 minutes

Ingredients:

- 1 large zucchini
- 1/4 cup Italian-style salad dressing

- Smoke Time: 15 Mins
- Smoke Temp: 250

Directions:

1. Cut the zucchini up into ¼ inch slices. In a large bowl toss it with the Italian dressing.
2. Bring the smoker up to 250 degrees.
3. Place the zucchini in the smoker.
4. Serve and eat.

130. SMOKED YELLOW SQUASH

Servings: 4
Preparation Time: 15 minutes

Ingredients:

- 4 medium yellow squash
- 1/2 cup extra virgin olive oil
- 2 cloves garlic, crushed
- salt and pepper to taste
- Smoke Time: 25 Mins
- Smoke Temp: 250

Directions:

1. Cut your squash horizontally. Cut it into ¼ inch and ½ inch slices.
2. In a small pan heat up some garlic clove and olive oil over medium heat. Do this until the garlic starts to sizzle. Brush each slice of squash with this garlic oil. Add salt and pepper to taste.
3. Place the squash in the smoker on a rack. Flip it on its other side halfway through. Continue to brush with the garlic oil as needed.
4. Serve while still warm.

131. MINI SMOKED SAUSAGE WITH BACON WRAP

Preparation Time: 2 hours 10 minutes
Servings: 10

Ingredients:

- Sausages (2-lbs., 0.9-kgs)
- Bacon – 8 slices
- The Rub
- Brown sugar – ¼ cup
- The Heat
- Use Apple wood chips for smoking.

Directions:

1. Turn an electric smoker on and set the temperature to 200°F (93°C).
2. Cut the bacon into halves then set aside.
3. Cut the sausage into halves then rub with brown sugar.
4. Place a sheet of bacon on a flat surface then add a halved sausage on it.
5. Roll the bacon until the sausage is completely coated then prick with a toothpick.
6. Repeat with the remaining bacon and sausages.
7. Once the smoker is ready, arrange the bacon wrapped sausages on the smoker's rack then smoke for 2 hours.
8. Once it is done, remove from the smoker then arrange on a serving dish.
9. Serve and enjoy warm.

132. SMOKED TOMATO ORIGINAL

Preparation Time: 2 hours 10 minutes
Servings: 10

Ingredients:

- Fresh tomatoes (1.5-lbs., 0.7-kgs)
- The Spice
- Salt – 3 tablespoons
- The Heat
- Use Hickory wood chips for smoking.

Directions:

1. Turn an electric smoker on and set the time to 165°F (74°C).
2. Cut the tomatoes into halves then discard the seeds and the core.
3. Season the tomatoes with salt and once the smoker has reached the desired temperature, arrange the halved tomatoes on the smoker's rack with the skin side up.
4. Smoke the tomatoes until pliable then remove from the smoker.
5. Serve and enjoy the smoked tomatoes with a cup of cheesy dip.

133. SMOKED PORTOBELLO MUSHROOM

Preparation Time: 1 hour 40 minutes
Servings: 10

Ingredients:

- Portobello mushroom (1-lb., 0.5-kg)
- The Spice
- Worcestershire sauce – ¼ cup
- Melted butter – ¼ cup
- Garlic powder – 3 tablespoons
- Salt – 2 tablespoons
- Pepper – 2 teaspoons
- The Heat
- Use Apple wood chips for smoking.

Directions:

1. Turn an electric smoker on and set the time to 225°F (107°C)
2. Wash and clean the mushrooms then cut the stems. Set aside.
3. Place Worcestershire sauce and melted butter in a bowl then stir until incorporated.
4. Stir the mushrooms into the Worcestershire mixture then toss until the mushrooms are completely coated with the sauce mixture.
5. Sprinkle garlic powder, salt, and pepper over the mushrooms

then stir well.

6. Once the smoker has reached the desired temperature, arrange the seasoned mushrooms on the smoker's rack.
7. Set the time to an hour and a half and smoke the mushrooms.
8. In the last 10 minutes of smoking, brush the smoked mushrooms with the remaining butter mixture and continue smoking.
9. Once it is done, take the smoked mushrooms out of the smoker and transfer to a serving dish.
10. Serve and enjoy.

134. SMOKY BEANS BARBECUE

Preparation Time: 50 minutes
Servings: 10

Ingredients:

- Canned beans (1-lb., 0.4-kg)
- The Spice
- Barbecue sauce – ¾ cup
- Brown sugar - ¾ cup
- Ketchup – ½ cup
- Water – ½ cup
- Molasses – ¼ cup
- Chili powder – 2 tablespoons
- Black pepper – 2 teaspoons
- The Heat
- Use Apple wood chips for smoking.

Directions:

1. Turn an electric smoker to 225°F (107°C).
2. Place the entire ingredients in a pan then stir well. Bring to boil over medium heat.
3. Once the mixture is boiled, stir and remove from heat. Let it warm.
4. Transfer the boiled beans to a disposable aluminum pan then spread evenly.

5. When the smoker is ready, place the aluminum pan with beans in the smoker.
6. Cover the smoker and set the time to 45 minutes.
7. Once it is done, remove from heat and let the smoked beans warm for a few minutes.
8. Transfer to a serving dish then enjoy!

135. CHEESY STUFFED SMOKED BELL PEPPERS

Preparation Time: 1 Hour 20 minutes
Servings: 10

Ingredients:

- Bell peppers 10 (2-lb., 0.9-kg)
- Ground beef – 1 ½ cups
- Diced onion – 1 cup
- Diced mushroom – ½ cup
- Grated Mozzarella cheese – 1 ½ cups
- Cooked rice – 1 ½ cups
- The Spice
- Chopped parsley – 1 cup
- Garlic powder – 2 tablespoons
- The Heat
- Use Apple wood chips for smoking.

Directions:

1. Turn an electric smoker on and set the temperature to 250°F (121°C).
2. Preheat a skillet over medium heat then brown the ground beef.
3. Add diced onion and diced mushrooms then stir well. Remove from heat.
4. Stir cooked rice into the skillet then season with chopped parsley and garlic powder. Mix until combined.
5. Using a sharp knife cut the tops of the bell pepper.
6. Take the stems and the seeds out of the bell pepper cavities.
7. Fill the bell pepper with the rice mixture then sprinkle grated

Mozzarella cheese on top.
8. Once the smoker has reached the desired temperature, arrange the stuffed bell peppers on the smoker's rack.
9. Place an aluminum pan with water and add wood chips to the drawer.
10. Set the time to 60 minutes and smoke the stuffed bell peppers.
11. Once it is done, remove the smoked stuffed bell peppers from the smoker.
12. Let the smoked stuffed bell peppers rest for a few minutes then arrange on a serving dish.
13. Serve and enjoy.

136. SMOKED CARROTS WITH SWEET GLAZE

Preparation Time: 2 hours 10 minutes
Servings: 10

Ingredients:
- Fresh carrots (1.5-lbs., 0.7-kgs)
- The Spice
- Salt – ¼ cup
- Garlic powder – 2 tablespoons
- The Glaze
- Butter – ¼ cup
- Sliced shallots – 2 tablespoons
- Vegetable broth – ¼ cup
- Maple syrup – ¼ cup
- Brown sugar – 2 tablespoons
- Salt – ¼ teaspoon
- Pepper – ½ teaspoon
- The Heat
- Use Apple wood chips for smoking.

Directions:
1. Turn an electric smoker on to 250°F (121°C).
2. Combine salt with garlic powder then rub the carrots with the spice mixture. Place in a disposable aluminum pan.

3. Once the smoker is ready, place the aluminum pan on the smoker's rack then set the time to 2 hours.
4. Smoked the carrots and check the smoke regularly.
5. Meanwhile, place butter over medium heat.
6. Once the butter is melted, stir in sliced shallots and sauté until wilted and aromatic.
7. Pour vegetable broth into the skillet then add maple syrup, brown sugar, salt, and pepper. Stir well then remove from heat.
8. 30 minutes before the end of the smoking time glaze the carrots with the glaze mixture then continue smoking.
9. Once the carrots are done, remove from the smoker and transfer to a serving dish.
10. Serve and enjoy!

SPICE RUBS, SAUCES, BRINES, AND MARINADES

137. SPICY HICKORY BBQ SAUCE

Servings: 3 cups
Preparation Time: 30 minutes
Cooking Time: 30 minutes
Preferred Wood Chip: Hickory Chips

Ingredients:
- 1 small onion, chopped
- 2 garlic cloves, chopped
- 2 cups ketchup
- 1 cup water
- ½ cup molasses
- ½ cup apple cider vinegar
- 5 tablespoons granulated sugar
- 5 tablespoons packed brown sugar
- 1 tablespoon Worcestershire sauce

- 1 tablespoon freshly squeezed lemon juice
- 2 teaspoons hickory liquid smoke
- 1½ teaspoons freshly ground black pepper
- 1½ teaspoons dry mustard powder

Directions:

1. Set your Smoker to 225 degrees/F and add wood chips
2. Place a saucepan over medium heat
3. Stir in onion, garlic, ketchup, water, molasses, vinegar, sugars, Worcestershire sauce, lemon juice, liquid smoke, pepper, and mustard
4. Bring it to a boil
5. Pour sauce into a small metal bowl and transfer to the smoker, smoke for 30 minutes
6. Strain out chunks for a smoother sauce
7. Use as needed!

Nutrition Values:

Calories: 170
Fats: 2g
Carbs: 39g
Protein: 3g

138. HOT PEPPER AND VINEGAR BBQ SAUCE

Servings: 3 cups
Preparation Time: 10 minutes
Cooking Time: 30 minutes
Preferred Wood Chip: None

Ingredients:

- 2 cups ketchup
- 1 cup firmly packed light brown sugar
- 1 cup hot pepper vinegar sauce
- 2 tablespoons white vinegar
- 2 tablespoons salt
- 1 tablespoon chili powder
- 2 teaspoons freshly ground black pepper

- 1 teaspoon garlic powder
- 1 teaspoon cayenne pepper
- ½ teaspoon ground allspice

Directions:
1. Place a saucepan over medium heat
2. Add ketchup, brown sugar, vinegar sauce, white vinegar, salt, chili powder, pepper, garlic powder, cayenne, and allspice and bring the mixture to a boil
3. Reduce heat to low and simmer for 25 minutes
4. Use as needed!

139. LOVELY CHICKEN SPICE RUB

Serving: 2
Preparation Time: 50 minutes
Cooking Time: 1-2 hours
Preferred Wood Chip: Apple Chips

Ingredients:
- 1 teaspoon salt
- 4 teaspoons dried basil
- 4 teaspoons crushed dried rosemary
- 2 teaspoons garlic powder
- 1 teaspoon dry mustard powder
- 1 teaspoon paprika
- ¼ teaspoon ground black pepper
- ¼ teaspoon ground dried thyme
- ½ teaspoon celery seed
- 1 teaspoon dried parsley
- ½ teaspoon ground cumin
- ½ teaspoon cayenne pepper

Directions:
1. Set your Smoker to 220 degrees/F
2. Mix the spices together in a bowl
3. Use a cold smoker attachment and fire up the apple chips until the temperature reaches 100 degrees/F

4. Transfer the spice blend to an aluminum pie pan
5. Smoke for 1-2 hours
6. Store and use!

Nutrition Values:

Calories: 60
Fats: 2g
Carbs: 8g
Protein: 2g

140. EXOTIC RUB MIX

Serving: 2
Preparation Time: 1 hour
Cooking Time: 2 hours
Preferred Wood Chip: Apple Chips

Ingredients:

- ½ cup paprika
- ½ teaspoon brown sugar
- 2 tablespoons salt
- 4 tablespoons white pepper
- 4 tablespoons dry mustard powder

Directions:

1. Set your Smoker to 220 degrees/F
2. Mix the spices together in a bowl
3. Use a cold smoker attachment and fire up the apple chips until the temperature reaches 100 degrees/F
4. Transfer the spice blend to an aluminum pie pan
5. Smoke for 2 hours
6. Store and use!

Nutrition Values:

Calories: 280
Fats: 7g
Carbs: 56g
Protein: 8g

141. CHEESY COWBOY BUTTER

Serving: 1 cup
Preparation Time: 10 minutes + 4 hours chilling time
Cooking Time: Nil
Preferred Wood Chip: None

Ingredients:

- 1 cup unsalted butter, soft
- 4 ounces blue cheese, crumbled
- 1 teaspoon cayenne pepper
- ¼ cup scallions, chopped, white and green parts
- 1 teaspoon garlic powder
- 1 tablespoon brown sugar, firmly packed

Directions:

1. Cream the butter and cheese together in a food processor
2. Add cayenne pepper, garlic powder, scallions, and brown sugar and blend well
3. Using a sheet of wax paper, roll the mixture into a cylindrical log and wrap it well
4. Chill for 4 hours
5. Use as needed!

Nutrition Values:

Calories: 559
Fats: 45g
Carbs: 5g
Protein: 35g

142. GENTLE ALABAMA WHITE SAUCE

Serving: 1 cup
Preparation Time: 10 minutes
Cooking Time: Nil
Preferred Wood Chip: None

Ingredients:

- 1 cup mayonnaise

- ¼ cup apple cider vinegar
- 1 tablespoon hot chili powder
- 1 teaspoon Worcestershire sauce
- ½ teaspoon celery seeds
- ½ teaspoon red pepper flakes
- ¼ teaspoon cayenne pepper
- Salt and pepper to taste

Directions:

1. In a medium bowl, whisk together mayonnaise, vinegar, chili powder, Worcestershire sauce, celery seed, red pepper flakes, and cayenne
2. Season with salt and pepper
3. Whisk well
4. Use as needed

Nutrition Values:

Calories: 290
Fats: 5g
Carbs: 63g
Protein: 2g

143. THE GREAT CHIMICHURRI SAUCE

Serving: 1 cup
Preparation Time: 10 minutes
Cooking Time: Nil
Preferred Wood Chip: None

Ingredients:

- ½ cup olive oil
- 2 tablespoon fresh oregano leaves
- 2 tablespoons fresh parsley leaves, chopped
- 2 tablespoons garlic, minced
- 2 tablespoons red wine vinegar
- 2 teaspoons red pepper flakes
- Salt
- Freshly ground black pepper

Directions:

1. Add the listed ingredient (except salt and pepper) to a food processor and pulse until smooth
2. Season the mix with salt and pepper and pulse again
3. Use as needed

Nutrition Values:

Calories: 183
Fats: 18g
Carbs: 4g
Protein: 1g

144. THE BRILLIANT JAVA RUB

Serving: 1 cup
Preparation Time: 10 minutes
Cooking Time: Nil
Preferred Wood Chip: None

Ingredients:

- ¼ cup finely ground roasted coffee beans
- ¼ cup paprika
- ¼ cup garlic powder
- 2 tablespoons chili powder
- 1 tablespoon packed light brown sugar
- 1 tablespoon ground allspice
- 1 tablespoon ground coriander
- 1 tablespoon freshly ground black pepper
- 2 teaspoons dry mustard powder
- 1½ teaspoons celery seed

Directions:

1. Add ground coffee, paprika, garlic powder, chili powder, brown sugar, allspice, coriander, pepper, mustard, and celery seed to a blender
2. Pulse well until fine
3. Use as needed!

145. COOL SPICY RUB

Serving: 2
Preparation Time: 1 hour
Cooking Time: 1 hour
Preferred Wood Chip: Apple Chips

Ingredients:

- ½ tablespoon salt
- 4 teaspoons ground cayenne pepper
- 3 teaspoons ground white pepper
- 4 teaspoons ground black pepper
- 4 teaspoons paprika
- 4 teaspoons onion powder
- 3 teaspoons garlic powder

1. **Directions:**
2. Set your Smoker to 220 degrees/F
3. Mix the spices together in a bowl
4. Use a cold smoker attachment and fire up the apple chips until the temperature reaches 100 degrees/F
5. Transfer the spice blend to an aluminum pie pan
6. Smoke for 1 hour
7. Store and use!

Nutrition Values:
Calories: 32
Fats: 0.7g
Carbs: 7g
Protein: 1.4g

146. CREATIVE SMOKED SALT

Serving: 1 cup
Preparation Time: 30 minutes
Cooking Time: 1 hour
Preferred Wood Chip: Apple

Ingredients:

- ½ cup kosher salt

Directions:

1. Set your Smoker to 220 degrees/F, add wood chips
2. Use a cold smoker attachment and fire up the apple wood chips until the temperature reaches 100 degrees/F
3. Transfer ¼ cup kosher salt to an aluminum pie pan
4. Place in Smoker and smoke for an hour
5. Store in jar and use as needed!

147. SMOKED LEMON SALT

Servings: 125g
Preparation Time: 5 mins
Cooking Time: 1 hr. Ingredients:
Lemon salt

Directions:

1. Start by soaking your woodchips for around an hour and preheat your smoker to 350°F/175°C. Now take a thin sheet pan and sprinkle your lemon salt over the top. Make sure the layer is nice and even. Pop into your smoker for around an hour.

Nutrition Value:

Calories: 0Protein: 0g, Carbs: 0g, Fat: 0g

148. PINK PEPPERCORN SAUCE

Servings: 125g
Preparation Time: 5 mins
Cooking Time: 20 mins.

Ingredients:

- 2 Tbsp. red wine vinegar
- 2/3 cup (150ml) chicken stock
- 2 tsp. pink peppercorns, slightly crushed
- 4 Tbsp. double cream
- Salt and pepper, to taste

Directions:

1. Start by placing the red wine vinegar into a skillet and place over a medium heat until simmering. Next add the chicken stock, stir well and heat until the mixture reduces by half. Add the peppercorns and the cream, then stir well. Then simmer for a minute or so to allow the sauce to thicken. Season with salt and pepper to taste then serve and enjoy!

Nutrition Value:

Calories: 120Protein: 1.2g, Carbs: 3.2g, Fat: 0.1g

149. SMOKED RED PEPPERCORNS

Servings: 125g
Preparation Time: 5 mins
Cooking Time: 1 hr.

Ingredients:

- Red Peppercorns

Directions:

1. Start by soaking your woodchips for around an hour and preheat your smoker to 350°F/175°C. Now take a thin sheet pan and sprinkle your peppercorns over the top. Make sure the layer is nice and even. Pop into your smoker for around an hour.

Nutrition Value:

Calories: 0Protein: 0g, Carbs: 0g, Fat: 0g

150. SWEET SPICE RUB

Servings: 125g
Preparation Time: 5 mins
Cooking Time: 0 mins.

Ingredients:

- Brown sugar (¼ cup)
- Salt (1 tbsp.)
- Garlic powder (2 tsp.)

- Chili powder (1 tbsp.)
- Paprika (1 tbsp.)
- Onion powder (2 tsp.)
- Oregano (1 tsp.)

Directions:
1. Simply place all ingredients into an airtight jar, stir well to combine then close. Use within six months.
2. Calories: 10Protein: 1.2g, Carbs: 3.2g, Fat: 0.1g

151. PAPRIKA BBQ RUB

Servings: 125g
Preparation Time: 5 mins
Cooking Time: 0 hrs.

Ingredients:
- Salt (2 tbsp.)
- Black pepper (2 tbsp., ground)
- White sugar (2 tbsp.)
- Paprika (¼ cup)
- Brown sugar (2 tbsp.)
- Cumin (2 tbsp., ground)
- Chili powder (2 tbsp.)

Directions:
1. Simply place all ingredients into an airtight jar, stir well to combine then close. Use within six months.

Nutrition Value:
Calories: 30Protein: 1.6g, Carbs: 3.2g, Fat: 0.2g

152. SESAME & WHITE BEAN SAUCE

Servings: 125g
Preparation Time: 5 mins
Cooking Time: 0 hrs.

Ingredients:

- ½ can drained and rinsed white beans
- 1 tsp. soft dark brown sugar
- 2 tsp. honey
- 1 tsp. Chinese five-spice powder
- ½ tsp. grated ginger
- 1 red chili
- 2 tsp. tahini (sesame paste)
- 2 Tbsp. cider vinegar
- 2 tsp. soy sauce
- 5 Tbsp. water
- Salt and pepper, to taste

Directions:

1. Start by opening up your food processor and throwing in all the ingredients. Hit the button, blend until smooth then pour the sauce into a saucepan. Cook over a medium heat for 5 minutes until glossy and thick, stirring continuously.

Nutrition Value:

Calories: 10Protein: 1.2g, Carbs: 3.2g, Fat: 0.1g

153. BBQ SAGE RUB

Servings: 125g
Preparation Time: 5 mins
Cooking Time: 0 hrs.

Ingredients:

- ¾ cup (80g) paprika
- ½ cup (100g) sugar
- ½ cup (135g) salt
- ¼ cup (27g) ground black pepper
- 2 Tbsp. thyme
- 2 Tbsp. dry mustard
- 1 Tbsp. cumin
- 1 Tbsp. cayenne pepper
- 1 Tbsp. sage

Directions:

1. Simply place all ingredients into an airtight jar, stir well to combine then close. Use within six months.

Nutrition Value:

Calories: 40Protein: 3.2g, Carbs: 2.2g, Fat: 1g

154. CHILI CHIPOTLE SAUCE

Servings: 125g
Preparation Time: 5 mins
Cooking Time: 0 hrs.

Ingredients:

*   2 Tbsp. vinegar
*   Salt and pepper, to taste
*   Ginger, 1 Tbsp., sliced
*   Garlic, 1 clove, chopped
*   Olive oil, 1 Tbsp.
*   Cherry peppers, drained, 6 marinated
*   Red pepper, ½, chopped
*   San Marzano tomatoes, 4 whole, drained
*   Chipotle powder, ½ tsp.
*   Scallion, 1 large

Directions:

1. This one is very easy! Simply place all the ingredients into a food processor and blend until smooth. Serve and enjoy!

Nutrition Value:

Calories: 10Protein: 1.2g, Carbs: 3.2g, Fat: 0.1g

155. GREEN SALSA

Servings: 125g
Preparation Time: 5 mins
Cooking Time: 0 hrs.

Ingredients:

- Small bunch each of parsley, chives and mint
- 1 tsp. capers
- 2-3 anchovies, chopped
- 1 clove garlic, chopped
- Juice of one lemon
- 3 Tbsp. olive oil
- Salt and pepper, to taste

Directions:

1. Start by chopping the herbs into small pieces and place into a medium bowl. Add the capers, anchovies, garlic, lemon juice, and olive oil, then stir well to combine. Season with salt and pepper to taste then serve and… enjoy!

Nutrition Value:

Calories: 50Protein: 4.2g, Carbs: 4.2g, Fat: 1.1g

156. RED WINE BEEF SAUCE

Servings: 125g
Preparation Time: 5 mins
Cooking Time: 0 hrs.

Ingredients:

- Beef stock (1 cup)
- Red wine (½ cup)
- Brown sugar (2 tsp., dark)
- Balsamic vinegar (1 tsp.)
- Salt and pepper, to taste

Directions:

1. Start by placing the beef stock into a saucepan and place over a medium heat. Simmer until reduced to half. Next add the remaining ingredients, then stir to combine. Continue cooking for another 10 minutes or so until the sauce has reduced to half again. Remove from the heat, season to taste then serve and enjoy!

Nutrition Value:

Calories: 10Protein: 1.2g, Carbs: 3.2g, Fat: 0.1g

1000-DAY MEAL PLAN

DAY	LUNCH	DINNER	SNACK
1	Smoked Burgers	Smoked Fish in a Brine	Smoked Dessert Pizza
2	Authentic Citrus Smoked Chicken	Smoked Green Beans with Lemon	Beef Jerky
3	Simple Salt & Pepper Smoked Salmon	Smoked Ultimate Flank Steak	Venison Rolls
4	Basic Brisket	Amazing Mesquite Maple And Bacon Chicken	Hamburger Jerky
5	Memphis Style Beef Ribs	Herby Smoked Cauliflower	Smokey Pimento Cheese Appetizer
6	Smoked Summer Vegetables	Smoked Salmon	Sweet Tea Pork Jerky
7	Fully Smoked Herbal Quail	Slow Smoked Porterhouse Steaks	Pork Belly Burnt Ends
8	Smoked Steak Strips	Smoked Paprika Chicken	White Chocolate Bread Pudding
9	Smoked Fish with the Delicious Dip	Smoky Corn on the Cob	Roasted Pears
10	Smoked Lemony-Garlic Artichokes	Ultimate Chuck Roast	Smoke Roasted Apple Crisp
11	Sweet Cola Ribs	Classic Smoke Trout	Tangerine Smoked Flans
12	Honey Smoked Turkey	Smoked Squash Casserole	Smoked Peach Crumble
13	Pineapple Maple Glaze Fish In the Smoker	Curiously Smoked Italian Sausages	Baked Lemon Meringue Pie
14	Juicy Glaze Ham	Standing Smoked Chicken	Pork Tenderloin Appetizers
15	Smoked Potato Salad	Groovy smoked asparagus	Teriyaki Smoked Venison Jerky
16	Smoked Buffalo Chicken Wings	The Spacious Home Made Bacon	Summer Sausage
17	Strawberry and Jalapeno Smoked Ribs	Smoked Catfish Recipe	Stout Beef Jerky
18	Smoked Tuna	Smoked Eggplant	Jalapeno Poppers
19	Smoked Eel	Orange Smoked Chicken	Tri-Tip Roast and Horseradish Chevre Crostini
20	Smoked Portobello	Delicious Maple Glazed	Candied Bacon

	Mushrooms with Herbs de Provence	Smoked Bacon	
21	Crazy Smoked Pork Spare Ribs	Smoked Volcano Potatoes	Chex Mix
22	Easy-Peasy Smoked Ribs	Tender Sweet Sriracha BBQ Chicken	Upside Down Cake
23	Supreme Chipotle Wings	Damn Feisty Pork Butt	Smoked Plums
24	Twice Pulled Potatoes	Honey Mustard Halibut Fillets	Plum Pie
25	Smoked "Onion Soup" Pork	Orange Crispy Chicken	Nutty Chocolate Bananas
26	Equally Worthy Cinnamon Cured Smoked Chicken	Slow Smoked Porterhouse Steaks	Bacon Wraps
27	Smoked Burgers	Smoked Fish in a Brine	Smoked Dessert Pizza
28	Authentic Citrus Smoked Chicken	Smoked Green Beans with Lemon	Beef Jerky
29	Simple Salt & Pepper Smoked Salmon	Smoked Ultimate Flank Steak	Venison Rolls
30	Basic Brisket	Amazing Mesquite Maple And Bacon Chicken	Hamburger Jerky
31	Memphis Style Beef Ribs	Herby Smoked Cauliflower	Smokey Pimento Cheese Appetizer
32	Smoked Summer Vegetables	Smoked Salmon	Sweet Tea Pork Jerky
33	Fully Smoked Herbal Quail	Slow Smoked Porterhouse Steaks	Pork Belly Burnt Ends
34	Smoked Steak Strips	Smoked Paprika Chicken	White Chocolate Bread Pudding
35	Smoked Fish with the Delicious Dip	Smoky Corn on the Cob	Roasted Pears
36	Smoked Lemony-Garlic Artichokes	Ultimate Chuck Roast	Smoke Roasted Apple Crisp
37	Sweet Cola Ribs	Classic Smoke Trout	Tangerine Smoked Flans
38	Honey Smoked Turkey	Smoked Squash Casserole	Smoked Peach Crumble
39	Pineapple Maple Glaze Fish In the Smoker	Curiously Smoked Italian Sausages	Baked Lemon Meringue Pie
40	Juicy Glaze Ham	Standing Smoked Chicken	Pork Tenderloin Appetizers
41	Smoked Potato Salad	Groovy smoked asparagus	Teriyaki Smoked Venison Jerky
42	Smoked Buffalo Chicken Wings	The Spacious Home Made Bacon	Summer Sausage
43	Strawberry and Jalapeno	Smoked Catfish Recipe	Stout Beef Jerky

	Smoked Ribs		
44	Smoked Tuna	Smoked Eggplant	Jalapeno Poppers
45	Smoked Eel	Orange Smoked Chicken	Tri-Tip Roast and Horseradish Chevre Crostini
46	Smoked Portobello Mushrooms with Herbs de Provence	Delicious Maple Glazed Smoked Bacon	Candied Bacon
47	Crazy Smoked Pork Spare Ribs	Smoked Volcano Potatoes	Chex Mix
48	Easy-Peasy Smoked Ribs	Tender Sweet Sriracha BBQ Chicken	Upside Down Cake
49	Supreme Chipotle Wings	Damn Feisty Pork Butt	Smoked Plums
50	Twice Pulled Potatoes	Honey Mustard Halibut Fillets	Plum Pie
51	Smoked "Onion Soup" Pork	Orange Crispy Chicken	Nutty Chocolate Bananas
52	Equally Worthy Cinnamon Cured Smoked Chicken	Slow Smoked Porterhouse Steaks	Bacon Wraps
53	Smoked Burgers	Smoked Fish in a Brine	Smoked Dessert Pizza
54	Authentic Citrus Smoked Chicken	Smoked Green Beans with Lemon	Beef Jerky
55	Simple Salt & Pepper Smoked Salmon	Smoked Ultimate Flank Steak	Venison Rolls
56	Basic Brisket	Amazing Mesquite Maple And Bacon Chicken	Hamburger Jerky
57	Memphis Style Beef Ribs	Herby Smoked Cauliflower	Smokey Pimento Cheese Appetizer
58	Smoked Summer Vegetables	Smoked Salmon	Sweet Tea Pork Jerky
59	Fully Smoked Herbal Quail	Slow Smoked Porterhouse Steaks	Pork Belly Burnt Ends
60	Smoked Steak Strips	Smoked Paprika Chicken	White Chocolate Bread Pudding
61	Smoked Fish with the Delicious Dip	Smoky Corn on the Cob	Roasted Pears
62	Smoked Lemony-Garlic Artichokes	Ultimate Chuck Roast	Smoke Roasted Apple Crisp
63	Sweet Cola Ribs	Classic Smoke Trout	Tangerine Smoked Flans
64	Honey Smoked Turkey	Smoked Squash Casserole	Smoked Peach Crumble
65	Pineapple Maple Glaze Fish In the Smoker	Curiously Smoked Italian Sausages	Baked Lemon Meringue Pie

66	Juicy Glaze Ham	Standing Smoked Chicken	Pork Tenderloin Appetizers
67	Smoked Potato Salad	Groovy smoked asparagus	Teriyaki Smoked Venison Jerky
68	Smoked Buffalo Chicken Wings	The Spacious Home Made Bacon	Summer Sausage
69	Strawberry and Jalapeno Smoked Ribs	Smoked Catfish Recipe	Stout Beef Jerky
70	Smoked Tuna	Smoked Eggplant	Jalapeno Poppers
71	Smoked Eel	Orange Smoked Chicken	Tri-Tip Roast and Horseradish Chevre Crostini
72	Smoked Portobello Mushrooms with Herbs de Provence	Delicious Maple Glazed Smoked Bacon	Candied Bacon
73	Crazy Smoked Pork Spare Ribs	Smoked Volcano Potatoes	Chex Mix
74	Easy-Peasy Smoked Ribs	Tender Sweet Sriracha BBQ Chicken	Upside Down Cake
75	Supreme Chipotle Wings	Damn Feisty Pork Butt	Smoked Plums
76	Twice Pulled Potatoes	Honey Mustard Halibut Fillets	Plum Pie
77	Smoked "Onion Soup" Pork	Orange Crispy Chicken	Nutty Chocolate Bananas
78	Equally Worthy Cinnamon Cured Smoked Chicken	Slow Smoked Porterhouse Steaks	Bacon Wraps
79	Smoked Burgers	Smoked Fish in a Brine	Smoked Dessert Pizza
80	Authentic Citrus Smoked Chicken	Smoked Green Beans with Lemon	Beef Jerky
81	Simple Salt & Pepper Smoked Salmon	Smoked Ultimate Flank Steak	Venison Rolls
82	Basic Brisket	Amazing Mesquite Maple And Bacon Chicken	Hamburger Jerky
83	Memphis Style Beef Ribs	Herby Smoked Cauliflower	Smokey Pimento Cheese Appetizer
84	Smoked Summer Vegetables	Smoked Salmon	Sweet Tea Pork Jerky
85	Fully Smoked Herbal Quail	Slow Smoked Porterhouse Steaks	Pork Belly Burnt Ends
86	Smoked Steak Strips	Smoked Paprika Chicken	White Chocolate Bread Pudding
87	Smoked Fish with the Delicious Dip	Smoky Corn on the Cob	Roasted Pears
88	Smoked Lemony-Garlic Artichokes	Ultimate Chuck Roast	Smoke Roasted Apple Crisp

89	Sweet Cola Ribs	Classic Smoke Trout	Tangerine Smoked Flans
90	Honey Smoked Turkey	Smoked Squash Casserole	Smoked Peach Crumble
91	Pineapple Maple Glaze Fish In the Smoker	Curiously Smoked Italian Sausages	Baked Lemon Meringue Pie
92	Juicy Glaze Ham	Standing Smoked Chicken	Pork Tenderloin Appetizers
93	Smoked Potato Salad	Groovy smoked asparagus	Teriyaki Smoked Venison Jerky
94	Smoked Buffalo Chicken Wings	The Spacious Home Made Bacon	Summer Sausage
95	Strawberry and Jalapeno Smoked Ribs	Smoked Catfish Recipe	Stout Beef Jerky
96	Smoked Tuna	Smoked Eggplant	Jalapeno Poppers
97	Smoked Eel	Orange Smoked Chicken	Tri-Tip Roast and Horseradish Chevre Crostini
98	Smoked Portobello Mushrooms with Herbs de Provence	Delicious Maple Glazed Smoked Bacon	Candied Bacon
99	Crazy Smoked Pork Spare Ribs	Smoked Volcano Potatoes	Chex Mix
100	Easy-Peasy Smoked Ribs	Tender Sweet Sriracha BBQ Chicken	Upside Down Cake
101	Supreme Chipotle Wings	Damn Feisty Pork Butt	Smoked Plums
102	Twice Pulled Potatoes	Honey Mustard Halibut Fillets	Plum Pie
103	Smoked "Onion Soup" Pork	Orange Crispy Chicken	Nutty Chocolate Bananas
104	Equally Worthy Cinnamon Cured Smoked Chicken	Slow Smoked Porterhouse Steaks	Bacon Wraps
105	Smoked Burgers	Smoked Fish in a Brine	Smoked Dessert Pizza
106	Authentic Citrus Smoked Chicken	Smoked Green Beans with Lemon	Beef Jerky
107	Simple Salt & Pepper Smoked Salmon	Smoked Ultimate Flank Steak	Venison Rolls
108	Basic Brisket	Amazing Mesquite Maple And Bacon Chicken	Hamburger Jerky
109	Memphis Style Beef Ribs	Herby Smoked Cauliflower	Smokey Pimento Cheese Appetizer
110	Smoked Summer Vegetables	Smoked Salmon	Sweet Tea Pork Jerky
111	Fully Smoked Herbal Quail	Slow Smoked Porterhouse Steaks	Pork Belly Burnt Ends

112	Smoked Steak Strips	Smoked Paprika Chicken	White Chocolate Bread Pudding
113	Smoked Fish with the Delicious Dip	Smoky Corn on the Cob	Roasted Pears
114	Smoked Lemony-Garlic Artichokes	Ultimate Chuck Roast	Smoke Roasted Apple Crisp
115	Sweet Cola Ribs	Classic Smoke Trout	Tangerine Smoked Flans
116	Honey Smoked Turkey	Smoked Squash Casserole	Smoked Peach Crumble
117	Pineapple Maple Glaze Fish In the Smoker	Curiously Smoked Italian Sausages	Baked Lemon Meringue Pie
118	Juicy Glaze Ham	Standing Smoked Chicken	Pork Tenderloin Appetizers
119	Smoked Potato Salad	Groovy smoked asparagus	Teriyaki Smoked Venison Jerky
120	Smoked Buffalo Chicken Wings	The Spacious Home Made Bacon	Summer Sausage
121	Strawberry and Jalapeno Smoked Ribs	Smoked Catfish Recipe	Stout Beef Jerky
122	Smoked Tuna	Smoked Eggplant	Jalapeno Poppers
123	Smoked Eel	Orange Smoked Chicken	Tri-Tip Roast and Horseradish Chevre Crostini
124	Smoked Portobello Mushrooms with Herbs de Provence	Delicious Maple Glazed Smoked Bacon	Candied Bacon
125	Crazy Smoked Pork Spare Ribs	Smoked Volcano Potatoes	Chex Mix
126	Easy-Peasy Smoked Ribs	Tender Sweet Sriracha BBQ Chicken	Upside Down Cake
127	Supreme Chipotle Wings	Damn Feisty Pork Butt	Smoked Plums
128	Twice Pulled Potatoes	Honey Mustard Halibut Fillets	Plum Pie
129	Smoked "Onion Soup" Pork	Orange Crispy Chicken	Nutty Chocolate Bananas
130	Equally Worthy Cinnamon Cured Smoked Chicken	Slow Smoked Porterhouse Steaks	Bacon Wraps
131	Smoked Burgers	Smoked Fish in a Brine	Smoked Dessert Pizza
132	Authentic Citrus Smoked Chicken	Smoked Green Beans with Lemon	Beef Jerky
133	Simple Salt & Pepper Smoked Salmon	Smoked Ultimate Flank Steak	Venison Rolls
134	Basic Brisket	Amazing Mesquite Maple And Bacon Chicken	Hamburger Jerky

135	Memphis Style Beef Ribs	Herby Smoked Cauliflower	Smokey Pimento Cheese Appetizer
136	Smoked Summer Vegetables	Smoked Salmon	Sweet Tea Pork Jerky
137	Fully Smoked Herbal Quail	Slow Smoked Porterhouse Steaks	Pork Belly Burnt Ends
138	Smoked Steak Strips	Smoked Paprika Chicken	White Chocolate Bread Pudding
139	Smoked Fish with the Delicious Dip	Smoky Corn on the Cob	Roasted Pears
140	Smoked Lemony-Garlic Artichokes	Ultimate Chuck Roast	Smoke Roasted Apple Crisp
141	Sweet Cola Ribs	Classic Smoke Trout	Tangerine Smoked Flans
142	Honey Smoked Turkey	Smoked Squash Casserole	Smoked Peach Crumble
143	Pineapple Maple Glaze Fish In the Smoker	Curiously Smoked Italian Sausages	Baked Lemon Meringue Pie
144	Juicy Glaze Ham	Standing Smoked Chicken	Pork Tenderloin Appetizers
145	Smoked Potato Salad	Groovy smoked asparagus	Teriyaki Smoked Venison Jerky
146	Smoked Buffalo Chicken Wings	The Spacious Home Made Bacon	Summer Sausage
147	Strawberry and Jalapeno Smoked Ribs	Smoked Catfish Recipe	Stout Beef Jerky
148	Smoked Tuna	Smoked Eggplant	Jalapeno Poppers
149	Smoked Eel	Orange Smoked Chicken	Tri-Tip Roast and Horseradish Chevre Crostini
150	Smoked Portobello Mushrooms with Herbs de Provence	Delicious Maple Glazed Smoked Bacon	Candied Bacon
151	Crazy Smoked Pork Spare Ribs	Smoked Volcano Potatoes	Chex Mix
152	Easy-Peasy Smoked Ribs	Tender Sweet Sriracha BBQ Chicken	Upside Down Cake
153	Supreme Chipotle Wings	Damn Feisty Pork Butt	Smoked Plums
154	Twice Pulled Potatoes	Honey Mustard Halibut Fillets	Plum Pie
155	Smoked "Onion Soup" Pork	Orange Crispy Chicken	Nutty Chocolate Bananas
156	Equally Worthy Cinnamon Cured Smoked Chicken	Slow Smoked Porterhouse Steaks	Bacon Wraps
157	Smoked Burgers	Smoked Fish in a Brine	Smoked Dessert Pizza

158	Authentic Citrus Smoked Chicken	Smoked Green Beans with Lemon	Beef Jerky
159	Simple Salt & Pepper Smoked Salmon	Smoked Ultimate Flank Steak	Venison Rolls
160	Basic Brisket	Amazing Mesquite Maple And Bacon Chicken	Hamburger Jerky
161	Memphis Style Beef Ribs	Herby Smoked Cauliflower	Smokey Pimento Cheese Appetizer
162	Smoked Summer Vegetables	Smoked Salmon	Sweet Tea Pork Jerky
163	Fully Smoked Herbal Quail	Slow Smoked Porterhouse Steaks	Pork Belly Burnt Ends
164	Smoked Steak Strips	Smoked Paprika Chicken	White Chocolate Bread Pudding
165	Smoked Fish with the Delicious Dip	Smoky Corn on the Cob	Roasted Pears
166	Smoked Lemony-Garlic Artichokes	Ultimate Chuck Roast	Smoke Roasted Apple Crisp
167	Sweet Cola Ribs	Classic Smoke Trout	Tangerine Smoked Flans
168	Honey Smoked Turkey	Smoked Squash Casserole	Smoked Peach Crumble
169	Pineapple Maple Glaze Fish In the Smoker	Curiously Smoked Italian Sausages	Baked Lemon Meringue Pie
170	Juicy Glaze Ham	Standing Smoked Chicken	Pork Tenderloin Appetizers
171	Smoked Potato Salad	Groovy smoked asparagus	Teriyaki Smoked Venison Jerky
172	Smoked Buffalo Chicken Wings	The Spacious Home Made Bacon	Summer Sausage
173	Strawberry and Jalapeno Smoked Ribs	Smoked Catfish Recipe	Stout Beef Jerky
174	Smoked Tuna	Smoked Eggplant	Jalapeno Poppers
175	Smoked Eel	Orange Smoked Chicken	Tri-Tip Roast and Horseradish Chevre Crostini
176	Smoked Portobello Mushrooms with Herbs de Provence	Delicious Maple Glazed Smoked Bacon	Candied Bacon
177	Crazy Smoked Pork Spare Ribs	Smoked Volcano Potatoes	Chex Mix
178	Easy-Peasy Smoked Ribs	Tender Sweet Sriracha BBQ Chicken	Upside Down Cake
179	Supreme Chipotle Wings	Damn Feisty Pork Butt	Smoked Plums
180	Twice Pulled Potatoes	Honey Mustard Halibut	Plum Pie

			Fillets	
181	Smoked "Onion Soup" Pork	Orange Crispy Chicken		Nutty Chocolate Bananas
182	Equally Worthy Cinnamon Cured Smoked Chicken	Slow Smoked Porterhouse Steaks		Bacon Wraps
183	Smoked Burgers	Smoked Fish in a Brine		Smoked Dessert Pizza
184	Authentic Citrus Smoked Chicken	Smoked Green Beans with Lemon		Beef Jerky
185	Simple Salt & Pepper Smoked Salmon	Smoked Ultimate Flank Steak		Venison Rolls
186	Basic Brisket	Amazing Mesquite Maple And Bacon Chicken		Hamburger Jerky
187	Memphis Style Beef Ribs	Herby Smoked Cauliflower		Smokey Pimento Cheese Appetizer
188	Smoked Summer Vegetables	Smoked Salmon		Sweet Tea Pork Jerky
189	Fully Smoked Herbal Quail	Slow Smoked Porterhouse Steaks		Pork Belly Burnt Ends
190	Smoked Steak Strips	Smoked Paprika Chicken		White Chocolate Bread Pudding
191	Smoked Fish with the Delicious Dip	Smoky Corn on the Cob		Roasted Pears
192	Smoked Lemony-Garlic Artichokes	Ultimate Chuck Roast		Smoke Roasted Apple Crisp
193	Sweet Cola Ribs	Classic Smoke Trout		Tangerine Smoked Flans
194	Honey Smoked Turkey	Smoked Squash Casserole		Smoked Peach Crumble
195	Pineapple Maple Glaze Fish In the Smoker	Curiously Smoked Italian Sausages		Baked Lemon Meringue Pie
196	Juicy Glaze Ham	Standing Smoked Chicken		Pork Tenderloin Appetizers
197	Smoked Potato Salad	Groovy smoked asparagus		Teriyaki Smoked Venison Jerky
198	Smoked Buffalo Chicken Wings	The Spacious Home Made Bacon		Summer Sausage
199	Strawberry and Jalapeno Smoked Ribs	Smoked Catfish Recipe		Stout Beef Jerky
200	Smoked Tuna	Smoked Eggplant		Jalapeno Poppers
201	Smoked Eel	Orange Smoked Chicken		Tri-Tip Roast and Horseradish Chevre Crostini
202	Smoked Portobello Mushrooms with Herbs de Provence	Delicious Maple Glazed Smoked Bacon		Candied Bacon

203	Crazy Smoked Pork Spare Ribs	Smoked Volcano Potatoes	Chex Mix
204	Easy-Peasy Smoked Ribs	Tender Sweet Sriracha BBQ Chicken	Upside Down Cake
205	Supreme Chipotle Wings	Damn Feisty Pork Butt	Smoked Plums
206	Twice Pulled Potatoes	Honey Mustard Halibut Fillets	Plum Pie
207	Smoked "Onion Soup" Pork	Orange Crispy Chicken	Nutty Chocolate Bananas
208	Equally Worthy Cinnamon Cured Smoked Chicken	Slow Smoked Porterhouse Steaks	Bacon Wraps
209	Smoked Burgers	Smoked Fish in a Brine	Smoked Dessert Pizza
210	Authentic Citrus Smoked Chicken	Smoked Green Beans with Lemon	Beef Jerky
211	Simple Salt & Pepper Smoked Salmon	Smoked Ultimate Flank Steak	Venison Rolls
212	Basic Brisket	Amazing Mesquite Maple And Bacon Chicken	Hamburger Jerky
213	Memphis Style Beef Ribs	Herby Smoked Cauliflower	Smokey Pimento Cheese Appetizer
214	Smoked Summer Vegetables	Smoked Salmon	Sweet Tea Pork Jerky
215	Fully Smoked Herbal Quail	Slow Smoked Porterhouse Steaks	Pork Belly Burnt Ends
216	Smoked Steak Strips	Smoked Paprika Chicken	White Chocolate Bread Pudding
217	Smoked Fish with the Delicious Dip	Smoky Corn on the Cob	Roasted Pears
218	Smoked Lemony-Garlic Artichokes	Ultimate Chuck Roast	Smoke Roasted Apple Crisp
219	Sweet Cola Ribs	Classic Smoke Trout	Tangerine Smoked Flans
220	Honey Smoked Turkey	Smoked Squash Casserole	Smoked Peach Crumble
221	Pineapple Maple Glaze Fish In the Smoker	Curiously Smoked Italian Sausages	Baked Lemon Meringue Pie
222	Juicy Glaze Ham	Standing Smoked Chicken	Pork Tenderloin Appetizers
223	Smoked Potato Salad	Groovy smoked asparagus	Teriyaki Smoked Venison Jerky
224	Smoked Buffalo Chicken Wings	The Spacious Home Made Bacon	Summer Sausage
225	Strawberry and Jalapeno Smoked Ribs	Smoked Catfish Recipe	Stout Beef Jerky
226	Smoked Tuna	Smoked Eggplant	Jalapeno Poppers

227	Smoked Eel	Orange Smoked Chicken	Tri-Tip Roast and Horseradish Chevre Crostini
228	Smoked Portobello Mushrooms with Herbs de Provence	Delicious Maple Glazed Smoked Bacon	Candied Bacon
229	Crazy Smoked Pork Spare Ribs	Smoked Volcano Potatoes	Chex Mix
230	Easy-Peasy Smoked Ribs	Tender Sweet Sriracha BBQ Chicken	Upside Down Cake
231	Supreme Chipotle Wings	Damn Feisty Pork Butt	Smoked Plums
232	Twice Pulled Potatoes	Honey Mustard Halibut Fillets	Plum Pie
233	Smoked "Onion Soup" Pork	Orange Crispy Chicken	Nutty Chocolate Bananas
234	Equally Worthy Cinnamon Cured Smoked Chicken	Slow Smoked Porterhouse Steaks	Bacon Wraps
235	Smoked Burgers	Smoked Fish in a Brine	Smoked Dessert Pizza
236	Authentic Citrus Smoked Chicken	Smoked Green Beans with Lemon	Beef Jerky
237	Simple Salt & Pepper Smoked Salmon	Smoked Ultimate Flank Steak	Venison Rolls
238	Basic Brisket	Amazing Mesquite Maple And Bacon Chicken	Hamburger Jerky
239	Memphis Style Beef Ribs	Herby Smoked Cauliflower	Smokey Pimento Cheese Appetizer
240	Smoked Summer Vegetables	Smoked Salmon	Sweet Tea Pork Jerky
241	Fully Smoked Herbal Quail	Slow Smoked Porterhouse Steaks	Pork Belly Burnt Ends
242	Smoked Steak Strips	Smoked Paprika Chicken	White Chocolate Bread Pudding
243	Smoked Fish with the Delicious Dip	Smoky Corn on the Cob	Roasted Pears
244	Smoked Lemony-Garlic Artichokes	Ultimate Chuck Roast	Smoke Roasted Apple Crisp
245	Sweet Cola Ribs	Classic Smoke Trout	Tangerine Smoked Flans
246	Honey Smoked Turkey	Smoked Squash Casserole	Smoked Peach Crumble
247	Pineapple Maple Glaze Fish In the Smoker	Curiously Smoked Italian Sausages	Baked Lemon Meringue Pie
248	Juicy Glaze Ham	Standing Smoked Chicken	Pork Tenderloin Appetizers
249	Smoked Potato Salad	Groovy smoked	Teriyaki Smoked

			asparagus	Venison Jerky
250	Smoked Buffalo Chicken Wings	The Spacious Home Made Bacon	Summer Sausage
251	Strawberry and Jalapeno Smoked Ribs	Smoked Catfish Recipe	Stout Beef Jerky
252	Smoked Tuna	Smoked Eggplant	Jalapeno Poppers
253	Smoked Eel	Orange Smoked Chicken	Tri-Tip Roast and Horseradish Chevre Crostini
254	Smoked Portobello Mushrooms with Herbs de Provence	Delicious Maple Glazed Smoked Bacon	Candied Bacon
255	Crazy Smoked Pork Spare Ribs	Smoked Volcano Potatoes	Chex Mix
256	Easy-Peasy Smoked Ribs	Tender Sweet Sriracha BBQ Chicken	Upside Down Cake
257	Supreme Chipotle Wings	Damn Feisty Pork Butt	Smoked Plums
258	Twice Pulled Potatoes	Honey Mustard Halibut Fillets	Plum Pie
259	Smoked "Onion Soup" Pork	Orange Crispy Chicken	Nutty Chocolate Bananas
260	Equally Worthy Cinnamon Cured Smoked Chicken	Slow Smoked Porterhouse Steaks	Bacon Wraps
261	Smoked Burgers	Smoked Fish in a Brine	Smoked Dessert Pizza
262	Authentic Citrus Smoked Chicken	Smoked Green Beans with Lemon	Beef Jerky
263	Simple Salt & Pepper Smoked Salmon	Smoked Ultimate Flank Steak	Venison Rolls
264	Basic Brisket	Amazing Mesquite Maple And Bacon Chicken	Hamburger Jerky
265	Memphis Style Beef Ribs	Herby Smoked Cauliflower	Smokey Pimento Cheese Appetizer
266	Smoked Summer Vegetables	Smoked Salmon	Sweet Tea Pork Jerky
267	Fully Smoked Herbal Quail	Slow Smoked Porterhouse Steaks	Pork Belly Burnt Ends
268	Smoked Steak Strips	Smoked Paprika Chicken	White Chocolate Bread Pudding
269	Smoked Fish with the Delicious Dip	Smoky Corn on the Cob	Roasted Pears
270	Smoked Lemony-Garlic Artichokes	Ultimate Chuck Roast	Smoke Roasted Apple Crisp
271	Sweet Cola Ribs	Classic Smoke Trout	Tangerine Smoked Flans

272	Honey Smoked Turkey	Smoked Squash Casserole	Smoked Peach Crumble
273	Pineapple Maple Glaze Fish In the Smoker	Curiously Smoked Italian Sausages	Baked Lemon Meringue Pie
274	Juicy Glaze Ham	Standing Smoked Chicken	Pork Tenderloin Appetizers
275	Smoked Potato Salad	Groovy smoked asparagus	Teriyaki Smoked Venison Jerky
276	Smoked Buffalo Chicken Wings	The Spacious Home Made Bacon	Summer Sausage
277	Strawberry and Jalapeno Smoked Ribs	Smoked Catfish Recipe	Stout Beef Jerky
278	Smoked Tuna	Smoked Eggplant	Jalapeno Poppers
279	Smoked Eel	Orange Smoked Chicken	Tri-Tip Roast and Horseradish Chevre Crostini
280	Smoked Portobello Mushrooms with Herbs de Provence	Delicious Maple Glazed Smoked Bacon	Candied Bacon
281	Crazy Smoked Pork Spare Ribs	Smoked Volcano Potatoes	Chex Mix
282	Easy-Peasy Smoked Ribs	Tender Sweet Sriracha BBQ Chicken	Upside Down Cake
283	Supreme Chipotle Wings	Damn Feisty Pork Butt	Smoked Plums
284	Twice Pulled Potatoes	Honey Mustard Halibut Fillets	Plum Pie
285	Smoked "Onion Soup" Pork	Orange Crispy Chicken	Nutty Chocolate Bananas
286	Equally Worthy Cinnamon Cured Smoked Chicken	Slow Smoked Porterhouse Steaks	Bacon Wraps
287	Smoked Burgers	Smoked Fish in a Brine	Smoked Dessert Pizza
288	Authentic Citrus Smoked Chicken	Smoked Green Beans with Lemon	Beef Jerky
289	Simple Salt & Pepper Smoked Salmon	Smoked Ultimate Flank Steak	Venison Rolls
290	Basic Brisket	Amazing Mesquite Maple And Bacon Chicken	Hamburger Jerky
291	Memphis Style Beef Ribs	Herby Smoked Cauliflower	Smokey Pimento Cheese Appetizer
292	Smoked Summer Vegetables	Smoked Salmon	Sweet Tea Pork Jerky
293	Fully Smoked Herbal Quail	Slow Smoked Porterhouse Steaks	Pork Belly Burnt Ends
294	Smoked Steak Strips	Smoked Paprika Chicken	White Chocolate Bread Pudding

295	Smoked Fish with the Delicious Dip	Smoky Corn on the Cob	Roasted Pears
296	Smoked Lemony-Garlic Artichokes	Ultimate Chuck Roast	Smoke Roasted Apple Crisp
297	Sweet Cola Ribs	Classic Smoke Trout	Tangerine Smoked Flans
298	Honey Smoked Turkey	Smoked Squash Casserole	Smoked Peach Crumble
299	Pineapple Maple Glaze Fish In the Smoker	Curiously Smoked Italian Sausages	Baked Lemon Meringue Pie
300	Juicy Glaze Ham	Standing Smoked Chicken	Pork Tenderloin Appetizers
301	Smoked Potato Salad	Groovy smoked asparagus	Teriyaki Smoked Venison Jerky
302	Smoked Buffalo Chicken Wings	The Spacious Home Made Bacon	Summer Sausage
303	Strawberry and Jalapeno Smoked Ribs	Smoked Catfish Recipe	Stout Beef Jerky
304	Smoked Tuna	Smoked Eggplant	Jalapeno Poppers
305	Smoked Eel	Orange Smoked Chicken	Tri-Tip Roast and Horseradish Chevre Crostini
306	Smoked Portobello Mushrooms with Herbs de Provence	Delicious Maple Glazed Smoked Bacon	Candied Bacon
307	Crazy Smoked Pork Spare Ribs	Smoked Volcano Potatoes	Chex Mix
308	Easy-Peasy Smoked Ribs	Tender Sweet Sriracha BBQ Chicken	Upside Down Cake
309	Supreme Chipotle Wings	Damn Feisty Pork Butt	Smoked Plums
310	Twice Pulled Potatoes	Honey Mustard Halibut Fillets	Plum Pie
311	Smoked "Onion Soup" Pork	Orange Crispy Chicken	Nutty Chocolate Bananas
312	Equally Worthy Cinnamon Cured Smoked Chicken	Slow Smoked Porterhouse Steaks	Bacon Wraps
313	Smoked Burgers	Smoked Fish in a Brine	Smoked Dessert Pizza
314	Authentic Citrus Smoked Chicken	Smoked Green Beans with Lemon	Beef Jerky
315	Simple Salt & Pepper Smoked Salmon	Smoked Ultimate Flank Steak	Venison Rolls
316	Basic Brisket	Amazing Mesquite Maple And Bacon Chicken	Hamburger Jerky
317	Memphis Style Beef Ribs	Herby Smoked Cauliflower	Smokey Pimento Cheese Appetizer

318	Smoked Summer Vegetables	Smoked Salmon	Sweet Tea Pork Jerky
319	Fully Smoked Herbal Quail	Slow Smoked Porterhouse Steaks	Pork Belly Burnt Ends
320	Smoked Steak Strips	Smoked Paprika Chicken	White Chocolate Bread Pudding
321	Smoked Fish with the Delicious Dip	Smoky Corn on the Cob	Roasted Pears
322	Smoked Lemony-Garlic Artichokes	Ultimate Chuck Roast	Smoke Roasted Apple Crisp
323	Sweet Cola Ribs	Classic Smoke Trout	Tangerine Smoked Flans
324	Honey Smoked Turkey	Smoked Squash Casserole	Smoked Peach Crumble
325	Pineapple Maple Glaze Fish In the Smoker	Curiously Smoked Italian Sausages	Baked Lemon Meringue Pie
326	Juicy Glaze Ham	Standing Smoked Chicken	Pork Tenderloin Appetizers
327	Smoked Potato Salad	Groovy smoked asparagus	Teriyaki Smoked Venison Jerky
328	Smoked Buffalo Chicken Wings	The Spacious Home Made Bacon	Summer Sausage
329	Strawberry and Jalapeno Smoked Ribs	Smoked Catfish Recipe	Stout Beef Jerky
330	Smoked Tuna	Smoked Eggplant	Jalapeno Poppers
331	Smoked Eel	Orange Smoked Chicken	Tri-Tip Roast and Horseradish Chevre Crostini
332	Smoked Portobello Mushrooms with Herbs de Provence	Delicious Maple Glazed Smoked Bacon	Candied Bacon
333	Crazy Smoked Pork Spare Ribs	Smoked Volcano Potatoes	Chex Mix
334	Easy-Peasy Smoked Ribs	Tender Sweet Sriracha BBQ Chicken	Upside Down Cake
335	Supreme Chipotle Wings	Damn Feisty Pork Butt	Smoked Plums
336	Twice Pulled Potatoes	Honey Mustard Halibut Fillets	Plum Pie
337	Smoked "Onion Soup" Pork	Orange Crispy Chicken	Nutty Chocolate Bananas
338	Equally Worthy Cinnamon Cured Smoked Chicken	Slow Smoked Porterhouse Steaks	Bacon Wraps
339	Smoked Burgers	Smoked Fish in a Brine	Smoked Dessert Pizza
340	Authentic Citrus Smoked Chicken	Smoked Green Beans with Lemon	Beef Jerky

341	Simple Salt & Pepper Smoked Salmon	Smoked Ultimate Flank Steak	Venison Rolls
342	Basic Brisket	Amazing Mesquite Maple And Bacon Chicken	Hamburger Jerky
343	Memphis Style Beef Ribs	Herby Smoked Cauliflower	Smokey Pimento Cheese Appetizer
344	Smoked Summer Vegetables	Smoked Salmon	Sweet Tea Pork Jerky
345	Fully Smoked Herbal Quail	Slow Smoked Porterhouse Steaks	Pork Belly Burnt Ends
346	Smoked Steak Strips	Smoked Paprika Chicken	White Chocolate Bread Pudding
347	Smoked Fish with the Delicious Dip	Smoky Corn on the Cob	Roasted Pears
348	Smoked Lemony-Garlic Artichokes	Ultimate Chuck Roast	Smoke Roasted Apple Crisp
349	Sweet Cola Ribs	Classic Smoke Trout	Tangerine Smoked Flans
350	Honey Smoked Turkey	Smoked Squash Casserole	Smoked Peach Crumble
351	Pineapple Maple Glaze Fish In the Smoker	Curiously Smoked Italian Sausages	Baked Lemon Meringue Pie
352	Juicy Glaze Ham	Standing Smoked Chicken	Pork Tenderloin Appetizers
353	Smoked Potato Salad	Groovy smoked asparagus	Teriyaki Smoked Venison Jerky
354	Smoked Buffalo Chicken Wings	The Spacious Home Made Bacon	Summer Sausage
355	Strawberry and Jalapeno Smoked Ribs	Smoked Catfish Recipe	Stout Beef Jerky
356	Smoked Tuna	Smoked Eggplant	Jalapeno Poppers
357	Smoked Eel	Orange Smoked Chicken	Tri-Tip Roast and Horseradish Chevre Crostini
358	Smoked Portobello Mushrooms with Herbs de Provence	Delicious Maple Glazed Smoked Bacon	Candied Bacon
359	Crazy Smoked Pork Spare Ribs	Smoked Volcano Potatoes	Chex Mix
360	Easy-Peasy Smoked Ribs	Tender Sweet Sriracha BBQ Chicken	Upside Down Cake
361	Supreme Chipotle Wings	Damn Feisty Pork Butt	Smoked Plums
362	Twice Pulled Potatoes	Honey Mustard Halibut Fillets	Plum Pie
363	Smoked "Onion Soup"	Orange Crispy Chicken	Nutty Chocolate

	Pork		Bananas
364	Equally Worthy Cinnamon Cured Smoked Chicken	Slow Smoked Porterhouse Steaks	Bacon Wraps
365	Smoked Burgers	Smoked Fish in a Brine	Smoked Dessert Pizza
366	Authentic Citrus Smoked Chicken	Smoked Green Beans with Lemon	Beef Jerky
367	Simple Salt & Pepper Smoked Salmon	Smoked Ultimate Flank Steak	Venison Rolls
368	Basic Brisket	Amazing Mesquite Maple And Bacon Chicken	Hamburger Jerky
369	Memphis Style Beef Ribs	Herby Smoked Cauliflower	Smokey Pimento Cheese Appetizer
370	Smoked Summer Vegetables	Smoked Salmon	Sweet Tea Pork Jerky
371	Fully Smoked Herbal Quail	Slow Smoked Porterhouse Steaks	Pork Belly Burnt Ends
372	Smoked Steak Strips	Smoked Paprika Chicken	White Chocolate Bread Pudding
373	Smoked Fish with the Delicious Dip	Smoky Corn on the Cob	Roasted Pears
374	Smoked Lemony-Garlic Artichokes	Ultimate Chuck Roast	Smoke Roasted Apple Crisp
375	Sweet Cola Ribs	Classic Smoke Trout	Tangerine Smoked Flans
376	Honey Smoked Turkey	Smoked Squash Casserole	Smoked Peach Crumble
377	Pineapple Maple Glaze Fish In the Smoker	Curiously Smoked Italian Sausages	Baked Lemon Meringue Pie
378	Juicy Glaze Ham	Standing Smoked Chicken	Pork Tenderloin Appetizers
379	Smoked Potato Salad	Groovy smoked asparagus	Teriyaki Smoked Venison Jerky
380	Smoked Buffalo Chicken Wings	The Spacious Home Made Bacon	Summer Sausage
381	Strawberry and Jalapeno Smoked Ribs	Smoked Catfish Recipe	Stout Beef Jerky
382	Smoked Tuna	Smoked Eggplant	Jalapeno Poppers
383	Smoked Eel	Orange Smoked Chicken	Tri-Tip Roast and Horseradish Chevre Crostini
384	Smoked Portobello Mushrooms with Herbs de Provence	Delicious Maple Glazed Smoked Bacon	Candied Bacon
385	Crazy Smoked Pork Spare Ribs	Smoked Volcano Potatoes	Chex Mix

386	Easy-Peasy Smoked Ribs	Tender Sweet Sriracha BBQ Chicken	Upside Down Cake
387	Supreme Chipotle Wings	Damn Feisty Pork Butt	Smoked Plums
388	Twice Pulled Potatoes	Honey Mustard Halibut Fillets	Plum Pie
389	Smoked "Onion Soup" Pork	Orange Crispy Chicken	Nutty Chocolate Bananas
390	Equally Worthy Cinnamon Cured Smoked Chicken	Slow Smoked Porterhouse Steaks	Bacon Wraps
391	Smoked Burgers	Smoked Fish in a Brine	Smoked Dessert Pizza
392	Authentic Citrus Smoked Chicken	Smoked Green Beans with Lemon	Beef Jerky
393	Simple Salt & Pepper Smoked Salmon	Smoked Ultimate Flank Steak	Venison Rolls
394	Basic Brisket	Amazing Mesquite Maple And Bacon Chicken	Hamburger Jerky
395	Memphis Style Beef Ribs	Herby Smoked Cauliflower	Smokey Pimento Cheese Appetizer
396	Smoked Summer Vegetables	Smoked Salmon	Sweet Tea Pork Jerky
397	Fully Smoked Herbal Quail	Slow Smoked Porterhouse Steaks	Pork Belly Burnt Ends
398	Smoked Steak Strips	Smoked Paprika Chicken	White Chocolate Bread Pudding
399	Smoked Fish with the Delicious Dip	Smoky Corn on the Cob	Roasted Pears
400	Smoked Lemony-Garlic Artichokes	Ultimate Chuck Roast	Smoke Roasted Apple Crisp
401	Sweet Cola Ribs	Classic Smoke Trout	Tangerine Smoked Flans
402	Honey Smoked Turkey	Smoked Squash Casserole	Smoked Peach Crumble
403	Pineapple Maple Glaze Fish In the Smoker	Curiously Smoked Italian Sausages	Baked Lemon Meringue Pie
404	Juicy Glaze Ham	Standing Smoked Chicken	Pork Tenderloin Appetizers
405	Smoked Potato Salad	Groovy smoked asparagus	Teriyaki Smoked Venison Jerky
406	Smoked Buffalo Chicken Wings	The Spacious Home Made Bacon	Summer Sausage
407	Strawberry and Jalapeno Smoked Ribs	Smoked Catfish Recipe	Stout Beef Jerky
408	Smoked Tuna	Smoked Eggplant	Jalapeno Poppers
409	Smoked Eel	Orange Smoked Chicken	Tri-Tip Roast and Horseradish Chevre

			Crostini
410	Smoked Portobello Mushrooms with Herbs de Provence	Delicious Maple Glazed Smoked Bacon	Candied Bacon
411	Crazy Smoked Pork Spare Ribs	Smoked Volcano Potatoes	Chex Mix
412	Easy-Peasy Smoked Ribs	Tender Sweet Sriracha BBQ Chicken	Upside Down Cake
413	Supreme Chipotle Wings	Damn Feisty Pork Butt	Smoked Plums
414	Twice Pulled Potatoes	Honey Mustard Halibut Fillets	Plum Pie
415	Smoked "Onion Soup" Pork	Orange Crispy Chicken	Nutty Chocolate Bananas
416	Equally Worthy Cinnamon Cured Smoked Chicken	Slow Smoked Porterhouse Steaks	Bacon Wraps
417	Smoked Burgers	Smoked Fish in a Brine	Smoked Dessert Pizza
418	Authentic Citrus Smoked Chicken	Smoked Green Beans with Lemon	Beef Jerky
419	Simple Salt & Pepper Smoked Salmon	Smoked Ultimate Flank Steak	Venison Rolls
420	Basic Brisket	Amazing Mesquite Maple And Bacon Chicken	Hamburger Jerky
421	Memphis Style Beef Ribs	Herby Smoked Cauliflower	Smokey Pimento Cheese Appetizer
422	Smoked Summer Vegetables	Smoked Salmon	Sweet Tea Pork Jerky
423	Fully Smoked Herbal Quail	Slow Smoked Porterhouse Steaks	Pork Belly Burnt Ends
424	Smoked Steak Strips	Smoked Paprika Chicken	White Chocolate Bread Pudding
425	Smoked Fish with the Delicious Dip	Smoky Corn on the Cob	Roasted Pears
426	Smoked Lemony-Garlic Artichokes	Ultimate Chuck Roast	Smoke Roasted Apple Crisp
427	Sweet Cola Ribs	Classic Smoke Trout	Tangerine Smoked Flans
428	Honey Smoked Turkey	Smoked Squash Casserole	Smoked Peach Crumble
429	Pineapple Maple Glaze Fish In the Smoker	Curiously Smoked Italian Sausages	Baked Lemon Meringue Pie
430	Juicy Glaze Ham	Standing Smoked Chicken	Pork Tenderloin Appetizers
431	Smoked Potato Salad	Groovy smoked asparagus	Teriyaki Smoked Venison Jerky

432	Smoked Buffalo Chicken Wings	The Spacious Home Made Bacon	Summer Sausage
433	Strawberry and Jalapeno Smoked Ribs	Smoked Catfish Recipe	Stout Beef Jerky
434	Smoked Tuna	Smoked Eggplant	Jalapeno Poppers
435	Smoked Eel	Orange Smoked Chicken	Tri-Tip Roast and Horseradish Chevre Crostini
436	Smoked Portobello Mushrooms with Herbs de Provence	Delicious Maple Glazed Smoked Bacon	Candied Bacon
437	Crazy Smoked Pork Spare Ribs	Smoked Volcano Potatoes	Chex Mix
438	Easy-Peasy Smoked Ribs	Tender Sweet Sriracha BBQ Chicken	Upside Down Cake
439	Supreme Chipotle Wings	Damn Feisty Pork Butt	Smoked Plums
440	Twice Pulled Potatoes	Honey Mustard Halibut Fillets	Plum Pie
441	Smoked "Onion Soup" Pork	Orange Crispy Chicken	Nutty Chocolate Bananas
442	Equally Worthy Cinnamon Cured Smoked Chicken	Slow Smoked Porterhouse Steaks	Bacon Wraps
443	Smoked Burgers	Smoked Fish in a Brine	Smoked Dessert Pizza
444	Authentic Citrus Smoked Chicken	Smoked Green Beans with Lemon	Beef Jerky
445	Simple Salt & Pepper Smoked Salmon	Smoked Ultimate Flank Steak	Venison Rolls
446	Basic Brisket	Amazing Mesquite Maple And Bacon Chicken	Hamburger Jerky
447	Memphis Style Beef Ribs	Herby Smoked Cauliflower	Smokey Pimento Cheese Appetizer
448	Smoked Summer Vegetables	Smoked Salmon	Sweet Tea Pork Jerky
449	Fully Smoked Herbal Quail	Slow Smoked Porterhouse Steaks	Pork Belly Burnt Ends
450	Smoked Steak Strips	Smoked Paprika Chicken	White Chocolate Bread Pudding
451	Smoked Fish with the Delicious Dip	Smoky Corn on the Cob	Roasted Pears
452	Smoked Lemony-Garlic Artichokes	Ultimate Chuck Roast	Smoke Roasted Apple Crisp
453	Sweet Cola Ribs	Classic Smoke Trout	Tangerine Smoked Flans
454	Honey Smoked Turkey	Smoked Squash Casserole	Smoked Peach Crumble

455	Pineapple Maple Glaze Fish In the Smoker	Curiously Smoked Italian Sausages	Baked Lemon Meringue Pie
456	Juicy Glaze Ham	Standing Smoked Chicken	Pork Tenderloin Appetizers
457	Smoked Potato Salad	Groovy smoked asparagus	Teriyaki Smoked Venison Jerky
458	Smoked Buffalo Chicken Wings	The Spacious Home Made Bacon	Summer Sausage
459	Strawberry and Jalapeno Smoked Ribs	Smoked Catfish Recipe	Stout Beef Jerky
460	Smoked Tuna	Smoked Eggplant	Jalapeno Poppers
461	Smoked Eel	Orange Smoked Chicken	Tri-Tip Roast and Horseradish Chevre Crostini
462	Smoked Portobello Mushrooms with Herbs de Provence	Delicious Maple Glazed Smoked Bacon	Candied Bacon
463	Crazy Smoked Pork Spare Ribs	Smoked Volcano Potatoes	Chex Mix
464	Easy-Peasy Smoked Ribs	Tender Sweet Sriracha BBQ Chicken	Upside Down Cake
465	Supreme Chipotle Wings	Damn Feisty Pork Butt	Smoked Plums
466	Twice Pulled Potatoes	Honey Mustard Halibut Fillets	Plum Pie
467	Smoked "Onion Soup" Pork	Orange Crispy Chicken	Nutty Chocolate Bananas
468	Equally Worthy Cinnamon Cured Smoked Chicken	Slow Smoked Porterhouse Steaks	Bacon Wraps
469	Smoked Burgers	Smoked Fish in a Brine	Smoked Dessert Pizza
470	Authentic Citrus Smoked Chicken	Smoked Green Beans with Lemon	Beef Jerky
471	Simple Salt & Pepper Smoked Salmon	Smoked Ultimate Flank Steak	Venison Rolls
472	Basic Brisket	Amazing Mesquite Maple And Bacon Chicken	Hamburger Jerky
473	Memphis Style Beef Ribs	Herby Smoked Cauliflower	Smokey Pimento Cheese Appetizer
474	Smoked Summer Vegetables	Smoked Salmon	Sweet Tea Pork Jerky
475	Fully Smoked Herbal Quail	Slow Smoked Porterhouse Steaks	Pork Belly Burnt Ends
476	Smoked Steak Strips	Smoked Paprika Chicken	White Chocolate Bread Pudding
477	Smoked Fish with the Delicious Dip	Smoky Corn on the Cob	Roasted Pears

478	Smoked Lemony-Garlic Artichokes	Ultimate Chuck Roast	Smoke Roasted Apple Crisp
479	Sweet Cola Ribs	Classic Smoke Trout	Tangerine Smoked Flans
480	Honey Smoked Turkey	Smoked Squash Casserole	Smoked Peach Crumble
481	Pineapple Maple Glaze Fish In the Smoker	Curiously Smoked Italian Sausages	Baked Lemon Meringue Pie
482	Juicy Glaze Ham	Standing Smoked Chicken	Pork Tenderloin Appetizers
483	Smoked Potato Salad	Groovy smoked asparagus	Teriyaki Smoked Venison Jerky
484	Smoked Buffalo Chicken Wings	The Spacious Home Made Bacon	Summer Sausage
485	Strawberry and Jalapeno Smoked Ribs	Smoked Catfish Recipe	Stout Beef Jerky
486	Smoked Tuna	Smoked Eggplant	Jalapeno Poppers
487	Smoked Eel	Orange Smoked Chicken	Tri-Tip Roast and Horseradish Chevre Crostini
488	Smoked Portobello Mushrooms with Herbs de Provence	Delicious Maple Glazed Smoked Bacon	Candied Bacon
489	Crazy Smoked Pork Spare Ribs	Smoked Volcano Potatoes	Chex Mix
490	Easy-Peasy Smoked Ribs	Tender Sweet Sriracha BBQ Chicken	Upside Down Cake
491	Supreme Chipotle Wings	Damn Feisty Pork Butt	Smoked Plums
492	Twice Pulled Potatoes	Honey Mustard Halibut Fillets	Plum Pie
493	Smoked "Onion Soup" Pork	Orange Crispy Chicken	Nutty Chocolate Bananas
494	Equally Worthy Cinnamon Cured Smoked Chicken	Slow Smoked Porterhouse Steaks	Bacon Wraps
495	Smoked Burgers	Smoked Fish in a Brine	Smoked Dessert Pizza
496	Authentic Citrus Smoked Chicken	Smoked Green Beans with Lemon	Beef Jerky
497	Simple Salt & Pepper Smoked Salmon	Smoked Ultimate Flank Steak	Venison Rolls
498	Basic Brisket	Amazing Mesquite Maple And Bacon Chicken	Hamburger Jerky
499	Memphis Style Beef Ribs	Herby Smoked Cauliflower	Smokey Pimento Cheese Appetizer
500	Smoked Summer Vegetables	Smoked Salmon	Sweet Tea Pork Jerky

501	Fully Smoked Herbal Quail	Slow Smoked Porterhouse Steaks	Pork Belly Burnt Ends
502	Smoked Steak Strips	Smoked Paprika Chicken	White Chocolate Bread Pudding
503	Smoked Fish with the Delicious Dip	Smoky Corn on the Cob	Roasted Pears
504	Smoked Lemony-Garlic Artichokes	Ultimate Chuck Roast	Smoke Roasted Apple Crisp
505	Sweet Cola Ribs	Classic Smoke Trout	Tangerine Smoked Flans
506	Honey Smoked Turkey	Smoked Squash Casserole	Smoked Peach Crumble
507	Pineapple Maple Glaze Fish In the Smoker	Curiously Smoked Italian Sausages	Baked Lemon Meringue Pie
508	Juicy Glaze Ham	Standing Smoked Chicken	Pork Tenderloin Appetizers
509	Smoked Potato Salad	Groovy smoked asparagus	Teriyaki Smoked Venison Jerky
510	Smoked Buffalo Chicken Wings	The Spacious Home Made Bacon	Summer Sausage
511	Strawberry and Jalapeno Smoked Ribs	Smoked Catfish Recipe	Stout Beef Jerky
512	Smoked Tuna	Smoked Eggplant	Jalapeno Poppers
513	Smoked Eel	Orange Smoked Chicken	Tri-Tip Roast and Horseradish Chevre Crostini
514	Smoked Portobello Mushrooms with Herbs de Provence	Delicious Maple Glazed Smoked Bacon	Candied Bacon
515	Crazy Smoked Pork Spare Ribs	Smoked Volcano Potatoes	Chex Mix
516	Easy-Peasy Smoked Ribs	Tender Sweet Sriracha BBQ Chicken	Upside Down Cake
517	Supreme Chipotle Wings	Damn Feisty Pork Butt	Smoked Plums
518	Twice Pulled Potatoes	Honey Mustard Halibut Fillets	Plum Pie
519	Smoked "Onion Soup" Pork	Orange Crispy Chicken	Nutty Chocolate Bananas
520	Equally Worthy Cinnamon Cured Smoked Chicken	Slow Smoked Porterhouse Steaks	Bacon Wraps
521	Smoked Burgers	Smoked Fish in a Brine	Smoked Dessert Pizza
522	Authentic Citrus Smoked Chicken	Smoked Green Beans with Lemon	Beef Jerky
523	Simple Salt & Pepper Smoked Salmon	Smoked Ultimate Flank Steak	Venison Rolls

524	Basic Brisket	Amazing Mesquite Maple And Bacon Chicken	Hamburger Jerky
525	Memphis Style Beef Ribs	Herby Smoked Cauliflower	Smokey Pimento Cheese Appetizer
526	Smoked Summer Vegetables	Smoked Salmon	Sweet Tea Pork Jerky
527	Fully Smoked Herbal Quail	Slow Smoked Porterhouse Steaks	Pork Belly Burnt Ends
528	Smoked Steak Strips	Smoked Paprika Chicken	White Chocolate Bread Pudding
529	Smoked Fish with the Delicious Dip	Smoky Corn on the Cob	Roasted Pears
530	Smoked Lemony-Garlic Artichokes	Ultimate Chuck Roast	Smoke Roasted Apple Crisp
531	Sweet Cola Ribs	Classic Smoke Trout	Tangerine Smoked Flans
532	Honey Smoked Turkey	Smoked Squash Casserole	Smoked Peach Crumble
533	Pineapple Maple Glaze Fish In the Smoker	Curiously Smoked Italian Sausages	Baked Lemon Meringue Pie
534	Juicy Glaze Ham	Standing Smoked Chicken	Pork Tenderloin Appetizers
535	Smoked Potato Salad	Groovy smoked asparagus	Teriyaki Smoked Venison Jerky
536	Smoked Buffalo Chicken Wings	The Spacious Home Made Bacon	Summer Sausage
537	Strawberry and Jalapeno Smoked Ribs	Smoked Catfish Recipe	Stout Beef Jerky
538	Smoked Tuna	Smoked Eggplant	Jalapeno Poppers
539	Smoked Eel	Orange Smoked Chicken	Tri-Tip Roast and Horseradish Chevre Crostini
540	Smoked Portobello Mushrooms with Herbs de Provence	Delicious Maple Glazed Smoked Bacon	Candied Bacon
541	Crazy Smoked Pork Spare Ribs	Smoked Volcano Potatoes	Chex Mix
542	Easy-Peasy Smoked Ribs	Tender Sweet Sriracha BBQ Chicken	Upside Down Cake
543	Supreme Chipotle Wings	Damn Feisty Pork Butt	Smoked Plums
544	Twice Pulled Potatoes	Honey Mustard Halibut Fillets	Plum Pie
545	Smoked "Onion Soup" Pork	Orange Crispy Chicken	Nutty Chocolate Bananas
546	Equally Worthy Cinnamon	Slow Smoked	Bacon Wraps

	Cured Smoked Chicken	Porterhouse Steaks	
547	Smoked Burgers	Smoked Fish in a Brine	Smoked Dessert Pizza
548	Authentic Citrus Smoked Chicken	Smoked Green Beans with Lemon	Beef Jerky
549	Simple Salt & Pepper Smoked Salmon	Smoked Ultimate Flank Steak	Venison Rolls
550	Basic Brisket	Amazing Mesquite Maple And Bacon Chicken	Hamburger Jerky
551	Memphis Style Beef Ribs	Herby Smoked Cauliflower	Smokey Pimento Cheese Appetizer
552	Smoked Summer Vegetables	Smoked Salmon	Sweet Tea Pork Jerky
553	Fully Smoked Herbal Quail	Slow Smoked Porterhouse Steaks	Pork Belly Burnt Ends
554	Smoked Steak Strips	Smoked Paprika Chicken	White Chocolate Bread Pudding
555	Smoked Fish with the Delicious Dip	Smoky Corn on the Cob	Roasted Pears
556	Smoked Lemony-Garlic Artichokes	Ultimate Chuck Roast	Smoke Roasted Apple Crisp
557	Sweet Cola Ribs	Classic Smoke Trout	Tangerine Smoked Flans
558	Honey Smoked Turkey	Smoked Squash Casserole	Smoked Peach Crumble
559	Pineapple Maple Glaze Fish In the Smoker	Curiously Smoked Italian Sausages	Baked Lemon Meringue Pie
560	Juicy Glaze Ham	Standing Smoked Chicken	Pork Tenderloin Appetizers
561	Smoked Potato Salad	Groovy smoked asparagus	Teriyaki Smoked Venison Jerky
562	Smoked Buffalo Chicken Wings	The Spacious Home Made Bacon	Summer Sausage
563	Strawberry and Jalapeno Smoked Ribs	Smoked Catfish Recipe	Stout Beef Jerky
564	Smoked Tuna	Smoked Eggplant	Jalapeno Poppers
565	Smoked Eel	Orange Smoked Chicken	Tri-Tip Roast and Horseradish Chevre Crostini
566	Smoked Portobello Mushrooms with Herbs de Provence	Delicious Maple Glazed Smoked Bacon	Candied Bacon
567	Crazy Smoked Pork Spare Ribs	Smoked Volcano Potatoes	Chex Mix
568	Easy-Peasy Smoked Ribs	Tender Sweet Sriracha BBQ Chicken	Upside Down Cake

569	Supreme Chipotle Wings	Damn Feisty Pork Butt	Smoked Plums
570	Twice Pulled Potatoes	Honey Mustard Halibut Fillets	Plum Pie
571	Smoked "Onion Soup" Pork	Orange Crispy Chicken	Nutty Chocolate Bananas
572	Equally Worthy Cinnamon Cured Smoked Chicken	Slow Smoked Porterhouse Steaks	Bacon Wraps
573	Smoked Burgers	Smoked Fish in a Brine	Smoked Dessert Pizza
574	Authentic Citrus Smoked Chicken	Smoked Green Beans with Lemon	Beef Jerky
575	Simple Salt & Pepper Smoked Salmon	Smoked Ultimate Flank Steak	Venison Rolls
576	Basic Brisket	Amazing Mesquite Maple And Bacon Chicken	Hamburger Jerky
577	Memphis Style Beef Ribs	Herby Smoked Cauliflower	Smokey Pimento Cheese Appetizer
578	Smoked Summer Vegetables	Smoked Salmon	Sweet Tea Pork Jerky
579	Fully Smoked Herbal Quail	Slow Smoked Porterhouse Steaks	Pork Belly Burnt Ends
580	Smoked Steak Strips	Smoked Paprika Chicken	White Chocolate Bread Pudding
581	Smoked Fish with the Delicious Dip	Smoky Corn on the Cob	Roasted Pears
582	Smoked Lemony-Garlic Artichokes	Ultimate Chuck Roast	Smoke Roasted Apple Crisp
583	Sweet Cola Ribs	Classic Smoke Trout	Tangerine Smoked Flans
584	Honey Smoked Turkey	Smoked Squash Casserole	Smoked Peach Crumble
585	Pineapple Maple Glaze Fish In the Smoker	Curiously Smoked Italian Sausages	Baked Lemon Meringue Pie
586	Juicy Glaze Ham	Standing Smoked Chicken	Pork Tenderloin Appetizers
587	Smoked Potato Salad	Groovy smoked asparagus	Teriyaki Smoked Venison Jerky
588	Smoked Buffalo Chicken Wings	The Spacious Home Made Bacon	Summer Sausage
589	Strawberry and Jalapeno Smoked Ribs	Smoked Catfish Recipe	Stout Beef Jerky
590	Smoked Tuna	Smoked Eggplant	Jalapeno Poppers
591	Smoked Eel	Orange Smoked Chicken	Tri-Tip Roast and Horseradish Chevre Crostini

592	Smoked Portobello Mushrooms with Herbs de Provence	Delicious Maple Glazed Smoked Bacon	Candied Bacon
593	Crazy Smoked Pork Spare Ribs	Smoked Volcano Potatoes	Chex Mix
594	Easy-Peasy Smoked Ribs	Tender Sweet Sriracha BBQ Chicken	Upside Down Cake
595	Supreme Chipotle Wings	Damn Feisty Pork Butt	Smoked Plums
596	Twice Pulled Potatoes	Honey Mustard Halibut Fillets	Plum Pie
597	Smoked "Onion Soup" Pork	Orange Crispy Chicken	Nutty Chocolate Bananas
598	Equally Worthy Cinnamon Cured Smoked Chicken	Slow Smoked Porterhouse Steaks	Bacon Wraps
599	Smoked Burgers	Smoked Fish in a Brine	Smoked Dessert Pizza
600	Authentic Citrus Smoked Chicken	Smoked Green Beans with Lemon	Beef Jerky
601	Simple Salt & Pepper Smoked Salmon	Smoked Ultimate Flank Steak	Venison Rolls
602	Basic Brisket	Amazing Mesquite Maple And Bacon Chicken	Hamburger Jerky
603	Memphis Style Beef Ribs	Herby Smoked Cauliflower	Smokey Pimento Cheese Appetizer
604	Smoked Summer Vegetables	Smoked Salmon	Sweet Tea Pork Jerky
605	Fully Smoked Herbal Quail	Slow Smoked Porterhouse Steaks	Pork Belly Burnt Ends
606	Smoked Steak Strips	Smoked Paprika Chicken	White Chocolate Bread Pudding
607	Smoked Fish with the Delicious Dip	Smoky Corn on the Cob	Roasted Pears
608	Smoked Lemony-Garlic Artichokes	Ultimate Chuck Roast	Smoke Roasted Apple Crisp
609	Sweet Cola Ribs	Classic Smoke Trout	Tangerine Smoked Flans
610	Honey Smoked Turkey	Smoked Squash Casserole	Smoked Peach Crumble
611	Pineapple Maple Glaze Fish In the Smoker	Curiously Smoked Italian Sausages	Baked Lemon Meringue Pie
612	Juicy Glaze Ham	Standing Smoked Chicken	Pork Tenderloin Appetizers
613	Smoked Potato Salad	Groovy smoked asparagus	Teriyaki Smoked Venison Jerky
614	Smoked Buffalo Chicken Wings	The Spacious Home Made Bacon	Summer Sausage

615	Strawberry and Jalapeno Smoked Ribs	Smoked Catfish Recipe	Stout Beef Jerky
616	Smoked Tuna	Smoked Eggplant	Jalapeno Poppers
617	Smoked Eel	Orange Smoked Chicken	Tri-Tip Roast and Horseradish Chevre Crostini
618	Smoked Portobello Mushrooms with Herbs de Provence	Delicious Maple Glazed Smoked Bacon	Candied Bacon
619	Crazy Smoked Pork Spare Ribs	Smoked Volcano Potatoes	Chex Mix
620	Easy-Peasy Smoked Ribs	Tender Sweet Sriracha BBQ Chicken	Upside Down Cake
621	Supreme Chipotle Wings	Damn Feisty Pork Butt	Smoked Plums
622	Twice Pulled Potatoes	Honey Mustard Halibut Fillets	Plum Pie
623	Smoked "Onion Soup" Pork	Orange Crispy Chicken	Nutty Chocolate Bananas
624	Equally Worthy Cinnamon Cured Smoked Chicken	Slow Smoked Porterhouse Steaks	Bacon Wraps
625	Smoked Burgers	Smoked Fish in a Brine	Smoked Dessert Pizza
626	Authentic Citrus Smoked Chicken	Smoked Green Beans with Lemon	Beef Jerky
627	Simple Salt & Pepper Smoked Salmon	Smoked Ultimate Flank Steak	Venison Rolls
628	Basic Brisket	Amazing Mesquite Maple And Bacon Chicken	Hamburger Jerky
629	Memphis Style Beef Ribs	Herby Smoked Cauliflower	Smokey Pimento Cheese Appetizer
630	Smoked Summer Vegetables	Smoked Salmon	Sweet Tea Pork Jerky
631	Fully Smoked Herbal Quail	Slow Smoked Porterhouse Steaks	Pork Belly Burnt Ends
632	Smoked Steak Strips	Smoked Paprika Chicken	White Chocolate Bread Pudding
633	Smoked Fish with the Delicious Dip	Smoky Corn on the Cob	Roasted Pears
634	Smoked Lemony-Garlic Artichokes	Ultimate Chuck Roast	Smoke Roasted Apple Crisp
635	Sweet Cola Ribs	Classic Smoke Trout	Tangerine Smoked Flans
636	Honey Smoked Turkey	Smoked Squash Casserole	Smoked Peach Crumble
637	Pineapple Maple Glaze Fish In the Smoker	Curiously Smoked Italian Sausages	Baked Lemon Meringue Pie

638	Juicy Glaze Ham	Standing Smoked Chicken	Pork Tenderloin Appetizers
639	Smoked Potato Salad	Groovy smoked asparagus	Teriyaki Smoked Venison Jerky
640	Smoked Buffalo Chicken Wings	The Spacious Home Made Bacon	Summer Sausage
641	Strawberry and Jalapeno Smoked Ribs	Smoked Catfish Recipe	Stout Beef Jerky
642	Smoked Tuna	Smoked Eggplant	Jalapeno Poppers
643	Smoked Eel	Orange Smoked Chicken	Tri-Tip Roast and Horseradish Chevre Crostini
644	Smoked Portobello Mushrooms with Herbs de Provence	Delicious Maple Glazed Smoked Bacon	Candied Bacon
645	Crazy Smoked Pork Spare Ribs	Smoked Volcano Potatoes	Chex Mix
646	Easy-Peasy Smoked Ribs	Tender Sweet Sriracha BBQ Chicken	Upside Down Cake
647	Supreme Chipotle Wings	Damn Feisty Pork Butt	Smoked Plums
648	Twice Pulled Potatoes	Honey Mustard Halibut Fillets	Plum Pie
649	Smoked "Onion Soup" Pork	Orange Crispy Chicken	Nutty Chocolate Bananas
650	Equally Worthy Cinnamon Cured Smoked Chicken	Slow Smoked Porterhouse Steaks	Bacon Wraps
651	Smoked Burgers	Smoked Fish in a Brine	Smoked Dessert Pizza
652	Authentic Citrus Smoked Chicken	Smoked Green Beans with Lemon	Beef Jerky
653	Simple Salt & Pepper Smoked Salmon	Smoked Ultimate Flank Steak	Venison Rolls
654	Basic Brisket	Amazing Mesquite Maple And Bacon Chicken	Hamburger Jerky
655	Memphis Style Beef Ribs	Herby Smoked Cauliflower	Smokey Pimento Cheese Appetizer
656	Smoked Summer Vegetables	Smoked Salmon	Sweet Tea Pork Jerky
657	Fully Smoked Herbal Quail	Slow Smoked Porterhouse Steaks	Pork Belly Burnt Ends
658	Smoked Steak Strips	Smoked Paprika Chicken	White Chocolate Bread Pudding
659	Smoked Fish with the Delicious Dip	Smoky Corn on the Cob	Roasted Pears
660	Smoked Lemony-Garlic Artichokes	Ultimate Chuck Roast	Smoke Roasted Apple Crisp

661	Sweet Cola Ribs	Classic Smoke Trout	Tangerine Smoked Flans
662	Honey Smoked Turkey	Smoked Squash Casserole	Smoked Peach Crumble
663	Pineapple Maple Glaze Fish In the Smoker	Curiously Smoked Italian Sausages	Baked Lemon Meringue Pie
664	Juicy Glaze Ham	Standing Smoked Chicken	Pork Tenderloin Appetizers
665	Smoked Potato Salad	Groovy smoked asparagus	Teriyaki Smoked Venison Jerky
666	Smoked Buffalo Chicken Wings	The Spacious Home Made Bacon	Summer Sausage
667	Strawberry and Jalapeno Smoked Ribs	Smoked Catfish Recipe	Stout Beef Jerky
668	Smoked Tuna	Smoked Eggplant	Jalapeno Poppers
669	Smoked Eel	Orange Smoked Chicken	Tri-Tip Roast and Horseradish Chevre Crostini
670	Smoked Portobello Mushrooms with Herbs de Provence	Delicious Maple Glazed Smoked Bacon	Candied Bacon
671	Crazy Smoked Pork Spare Ribs	Smoked Volcano Potatoes	Chex Mix
672	Easy-Peasy Smoked Ribs	Tender Sweet Sriracha BBQ Chicken	Upside Down Cake
673	Supreme Chipotle Wings	Damn Feisty Pork Butt	Smoked Plums
674	Twice Pulled Potatoes	Honey Mustard Halibut Fillets	Plum Pie
675	Smoked "Onion Soup" Pork	Orange Crispy Chicken	Nutty Chocolate Bananas
676	Equally Worthy Cinnamon Cured Smoked Chicken	Slow Smoked Porterhouse Steaks	Bacon Wraps
677	Smoked Burgers	Smoked Fish in a Brine	Smoked Dessert Pizza
678	Authentic Citrus Smoked Chicken	Smoked Green Beans with Lemon	Beef Jerky
679	Simple Salt & Pepper Smoked Salmon	Smoked Ultimate Flank Steak	Venison Rolls
680	Basic Brisket	Amazing Mesquite Maple And Bacon Chicken	Hamburger Jerky
681	Memphis Style Beef Ribs	Herby Smoked Cauliflower	Smokey Pimento Cheese Appetizer
682	Smoked Summer Vegetables	Smoked Salmon	Sweet Tea Pork Jerky
683	Fully Smoked Herbal Quail	Slow Smoked Porterhouse Steaks	Pork Belly Burnt Ends

684	Smoked Steak Strips	Smoked Paprika Chicken	White Chocolate Bread Pudding
685	Smoked Fish with the Delicious Dip	Smoky Corn on the Cob	Roasted Pears
686	Smoked Lemony-Garlic Artichokes	Ultimate Chuck Roast	Smoke Roasted Apple Crisp
687	Sweet Cola Ribs	Classic Smoke Trout	Tangerine Smoked Flans
688	Honey Smoked Turkey	Smoked Squash Casserole	Smoked Peach Crumble
689	Pineapple Maple Glaze Fish In the Smoker	Curiously Smoked Italian Sausages	Baked Lemon Meringue Pie
690	Juicy Glaze Ham	Standing Smoked Chicken	Pork Tenderloin Appetizers
691	Smoked Potato Salad	Groovy smoked asparagus	Teriyaki Smoked Venison Jerky
692	Smoked Buffalo Chicken Wings	The Spacious Home Made Bacon	Summer Sausage
693	Strawberry and Jalapeno Smoked Ribs	Smoked Catfish Recipe	Stout Beef Jerky
694	Smoked Tuna	Smoked Eggplant	Jalapeno Poppers
695	Smoked Eel	Orange Smoked Chicken	Tri-Tip Roast and Horseradish Chevre Crostini
696	Smoked Portobello Mushrooms with Herbs de Provence	Delicious Maple Glazed Smoked Bacon	Candied Bacon
697	Crazy Smoked Pork Spare Ribs	Smoked Volcano Potatoes	Chex Mix
698	Easy-Peasy Smoked Ribs	Tender Sweet Sriracha BBQ Chicken	Upside Down Cake
699	Supreme Chipotle Wings	Damn Feisty Pork Butt	Smoked Plums
700	Twice Pulled Potatoes	Honey Mustard Halibut Fillets	Plum Pie
701	Smoked "Onion Soup" Pork	Orange Crispy Chicken	Nutty Chocolate Bananas
702	Equally Worthy Cinnamon Cured Smoked Chicken	Slow Smoked Porterhouse Steaks	Bacon Wraps
703	Smoked Burgers	Smoked Fish in a Brine	Smoked Dessert Pizza
704	Authentic Citrus Smoked Chicken	Smoked Green Beans with Lemon	Beef Jerky
705	Simple Salt & Pepper Smoked Salmon	Smoked Ultimate Flank Steak	Venison Rolls
706	Basic Brisket	Amazing Mesquite Maple And Bacon Chicken	Hamburger Jerky

707	Memphis Style Beef Ribs	Herby Smoked Cauliflower	Smokey Pimento Cheese Appetizer
708	Smoked Summer Vegetables	Smoked Salmon	Sweet Tea Pork Jerky
709	Fully Smoked Herbal Quail	Slow Smoked Porterhouse Steaks	Pork Belly Burnt Ends
710	Smoked Steak Strips	Smoked Paprika Chicken	White Chocolate Bread Pudding
711	Smoked Fish with the Delicious Dip	Smoky Corn on the Cob	Roasted Pears
712	Smoked Lemony-Garlic Artichokes	Ultimate Chuck Roast	Smoke Roasted Apple Crisp
713	Sweet Cola Ribs	Classic Smoke Trout	Tangerine Smoked Flans
714	Honey Smoked Turkey	Smoked Squash Casserole	Smoked Peach Crumble
715	Pineapple Maple Glaze Fish In the Smoker	Curiously Smoked Italian Sausages	Baked Lemon Meringue Pie
716	Juicy Glaze Ham	Standing Smoked Chicken	Pork Tenderloin Appetizers
717	Smoked Potato Salad	Groovy smoked asparagus	Teriyaki Smoked Venison Jerky
718	Smoked Buffalo Chicken Wings	The Spacious Home Made Bacon	Summer Sausage
719	Strawberry and Jalapeno Smoked Ribs	Smoked Catfish Recipe	Stout Beef Jerky
720	Smoked Tuna	Smoked Eggplant	Jalapeno Poppers
721	Smoked Eel	Orange Smoked Chicken	Tri-Tip Roast and Horseradish Chevre Crostini
722	Smoked Portobello Mushrooms with Herbs de Provence	Delicious Maple Glazed Smoked Bacon	Candied Bacon
723	Crazy Smoked Pork Spare Ribs	Smoked Volcano Potatoes	Chex Mix
724	Easy-Peasy Smoked Ribs	Tender Sweet Sriracha BBQ Chicken	Upside Down Cake
725	Supreme Chipotle Wings	Damn Feisty Pork Butt	Smoked Plums
726	Twice Pulled Potatoes	Honey Mustard Halibut Fillets	Plum Pie
727	Smoked "Onion Soup" Pork	Orange Crispy Chicken	Nutty Chocolate Bananas
728	Equally Worthy Cinnamon Cured Smoked Chicken	Slow Smoked Porterhouse Steaks	Bacon Wraps
729	Smoked Burgers	Smoked Fish in a Brine	Smoked Dessert Pizza

730	Authentic Citrus Smoked Chicken	Smoked Green Beans with Lemon	Beef Jerky
731	Simple Salt & Pepper Smoked Salmon	Smoked Ultimate Flank Steak	Venison Rolls
732	Basic Brisket	Amazing Mesquite Maple And Bacon Chicken	Hamburger Jerky
733	Memphis Style Beef Ribs	Herby Smoked Cauliflower	Smokey Pimento Cheese Appetizer
734	Smoked Summer Vegetables	Smoked Salmon	Sweet Tea Pork Jerky
735	Fully Smoked Herbal Quail	Slow Smoked Porterhouse Steaks	Pork Belly Burnt Ends
736	Smoked Steak Strips	Smoked Paprika Chicken	White Chocolate Bread Pudding
737	Smoked Fish with the Delicious Dip	Smoky Corn on the Cob	Roasted Pears
738	Smoked Lemony-Garlic Artichokes	Ultimate Chuck Roast	Smoke Roasted Apple Crisp
739	Sweet Cola Ribs	Classic Smoke Trout	Tangerine Smoked Flans
740	Honey Smoked Turkey	Smoked Squash Casserole	Smoked Peach Crumble
741	Pineapple Maple Glaze Fish In the Smoker	Curiously Smoked Italian Sausages	Baked Lemon Meringue Pie
742	Juicy Glaze Ham	Standing Smoked Chicken	Pork Tenderloin Appetizers
743	Smoked Potato Salad	Groovy smoked asparagus	Teriyaki Smoked Venison Jerky
744	Smoked Buffalo Chicken Wings	The Spacious Home Made Bacon	Summer Sausage
745	Strawberry and Jalapeno Smoked Ribs	Smoked Catfish Recipe	Stout Beef Jerky
746	Smoked Tuna	Smoked Eggplant	Jalapeno Poppers
747	Smoked Eel	Orange Smoked Chicken	Tri-Tip Roast and Horseradish Chevre Crostini
748	Smoked Portobello Mushrooms with Herbs de Provence	Delicious Maple Glazed Smoked Bacon	Candied Bacon
749	Crazy Smoked Pork Spare Ribs	Smoked Volcano Potatoes	Chex Mix
750	Easy-Peasy Smoked Ribs	Tender Sweet Sriracha BBQ Chicken	Upside Down Cake
751	Supreme Chipotle Wings	Damn Feisty Pork Butt	Smoked Plums
752	Twice Pulled Potatoes	Honey Mustard Halibut	Plum Pie

184

		Fillets	
753	Smoked "Onion Soup" Pork	Orange Crispy Chicken	Nutty Chocolate Bananas
754	Equally Worthy Cinnamon Cured Smoked Chicken	Slow Smoked Porterhouse Steaks	Bacon Wraps
755	Smoked Burgers	Smoked Fish in a Brine	Smoked Dessert Pizza
756	Authentic Citrus Smoked Chicken	Smoked Green Beans with Lemon	Beef Jerky
757	Simple Salt & Pepper Smoked Salmon	Smoked Ultimate Flank Steak	Venison Rolls
758	Basic Brisket	Amazing Mesquite Maple And Bacon Chicken	Hamburger Jerky
759	Memphis Style Beef Ribs	Herby Smoked Cauliflower	Smokey Pimento Cheese Appetizer
760	Smoked Summer Vegetables	Smoked Salmon	Sweet Tea Pork Jerky
761	Fully Smoked Herbal Quail	Slow Smoked Porterhouse Steaks	Pork Belly Burnt Ends
762	Smoked Steak Strips	Smoked Paprika Chicken	White Chocolate Bread Pudding
763	Smoked Fish with the Delicious Dip	Smoky Corn on the Cob	Roasted Pears
764	Smoked Lemony-Garlic Artichokes	Ultimate Chuck Roast	Smoke Roasted Apple Crisp
765	Sweet Cola Ribs	Classic Smoke Trout	Tangerine Smoked Flans
766	Honey Smoked Turkey	Smoked Squash Casserole	Smoked Peach Crumble
767	Pineapple Maple Glaze Fish In the Smoker	Curiously Smoked Italian Sausages	Baked Lemon Meringue Pie
768	Juicy Glaze Ham	Standing Smoked Chicken	Pork Tenderloin Appetizers
769	Smoked Potato Salad	Groovy smoked asparagus	Teriyaki Smoked Venison Jerky
770	Smoked Buffalo Chicken Wings	The Spacious Home Made Bacon	Summer Sausage
771	Strawberry and Jalapeno Smoked Ribs	Smoked Catfish Recipe	Stout Beef Jerky
772	Smoked Tuna	Smoked Eggplant	Jalapeno Poppers
773	Smoked Eel	Orange Smoked Chicken	Tri-Tip Roast and Horseradish Chevre Crostini
774	Smoked Portobello Mushrooms with Herbs de Provence	Delicious Maple Glazed Smoked Bacon	Candied Bacon

775	Crazy Smoked Pork Spare Ribs	Smoked Volcano Potatoes	Chex Mix
776	Easy-Peasy Smoked Ribs	Tender Sweet Sriracha BBQ Chicken	Upside Down Cake
777	Supreme Chipotle Wings	Damn Feisty Pork Butt	Smoked Plums
778	Twice Pulled Potatoes	Honey Mustard Halibut Fillets	Plum Pie
779	Smoked "Onion Soup" Pork	Orange Crispy Chicken	Nutty Chocolate Bananas
780	Equally Worthy Cinnamon Cured Smoked Chicken	Slow Smoked Porterhouse Steaks	Bacon Wraps
781	Smoked Burgers	Smoked Fish in a Brine	Smoked Dessert Pizza
782	Authentic Citrus Smoked Chicken	Smoked Green Beans with Lemon	Beef Jerky
783	Simple Salt & Pepper Smoked Salmon	Smoked Ultimate Flank Steak	Venison Rolls
784	Basic Brisket	Amazing Mesquite Maple And Bacon Chicken	Hamburger Jerky
785	Memphis Style Beef Ribs	Herby Smoked Cauliflower	Smokey Pimento Cheese Appetizer
786	Smoked Summer Vegetables	Smoked Salmon	Sweet Tea Pork Jerky
787	Fully Smoked Herbal Quail	Slow Smoked Porterhouse Steaks	Pork Belly Burnt Ends
788	Smoked Steak Strips	Smoked Paprika Chicken	White Chocolate Bread Pudding
789	Smoked Fish with the Delicious Dip	Smoky Corn on the Cob	Roasted Pears
790	Smoked Lemony-Garlic Artichokes	Ultimate Chuck Roast	Smoke Roasted Apple Crisp
791	Sweet Cola Ribs	Classic Smoke Trout	Tangerine Smoked Flans
792	Honey Smoked Turkey	Smoked Squash Casserole	Smoked Peach Crumble
793	Pineapple Maple Glaze Fish In the Smoker	Curiously Smoked Italian Sausages	Baked Lemon Meringue Pie
794	Juicy Glaze Ham	Standing Smoked Chicken	Pork Tenderloin Appetizers
795	Smoked Potato Salad	Groovy smoked asparagus	Teriyaki Smoked Venison Jerky
796	Smoked Buffalo Chicken Wings	The Spacious Home Made Bacon	Summer Sausage
797	Strawberry and Jalapeno Smoked Ribs	Smoked Catfish Recipe	Stout Beef Jerky
798	Smoked Tuna	Smoked Eggplant	Jalapeno Poppers

799	Smoked Eel	Orange Smoked Chicken	Tri-Tip Roast and Horseradish Chevre Crostini
800	Smoked Portobello Mushrooms with Herbs de Provence	Delicious Maple Glazed Smoked Bacon	Candied Bacon
801	Crazy Smoked Pork Spare Ribs	Smoked Volcano Potatoes	Chex Mix
802	Easy-Peasy Smoked Ribs	Tender Sweet Sriracha BBQ Chicken	Upside Down Cake
803	Supreme Chipotle Wings	Damn Feisty Pork Butt	Smoked Plums
804	Twice Pulled Potatoes	Honey Mustard Halibut Fillets	Plum Pie
805	Smoked "Onion Soup" Pork	Orange Crispy Chicken	Nutty Chocolate Bananas
806	Equally Worthy Cinnamon Cured Smoked Chicken	Slow Smoked Porterhouse Steaks	Bacon Wraps
807	Smoked Burgers	Smoked Fish in a Brine	Smoked Dessert Pizza
808	Authentic Citrus Smoked Chicken	Smoked Green Beans with Lemon	Beef Jerky
809	Simple Salt & Pepper Smoked Salmon	Smoked Ultimate Flank Steak	Venison Rolls
810	Basic Brisket	Amazing Mesquite Maple And Bacon Chicken	Hamburger Jerky
811	Memphis Style Beef Ribs	Herby Smoked Cauliflower	Smokey Pimento Cheese Appetizer
812	Smoked Summer Vegetables	Smoked Salmon	Sweet Tea Pork Jerky
813	Fully Smoked Herbal Quail	Slow Smoked Porterhouse Steaks	Pork Belly Burnt Ends
814	Smoked Steak Strips	Smoked Paprika Chicken	White Chocolate Bread Pudding
815	Smoked Fish with the Delicious Dip	Smoky Corn on the Cob	Roasted Pears
816	Smoked Lemony-Garlic Artichokes	Ultimate Chuck Roast	Smoke Roasted Apple Crisp
817	Sweet Cola Ribs	Classic Smoke Trout	Tangerine Smoked Flans
818	Honey Smoked Turkey	Smoked Squash Casserole	Smoked Peach Crumble
819	Pineapple Maple Glaze Fish In the Smoker	Curiously Smoked Italian Sausages	Baked Lemon Meringue Pie
820	Juicy Glaze Ham	Standing Smoked Chicken	Pork Tenderloin Appetizers
821	Smoked Potato Salad	Groovy smoked	Teriyaki Smoked

		asparagus	Venison Jerky
822	Smoked Buffalo Chicken Wings	The Spacious Home Made Bacon	Summer Sausage
823	Strawberry and Jalapeno Smoked Ribs	Smoked Catfish Recipe	Stout Beef Jerky
824	Smoked Tuna	Smoked Eggplant	Jalapeno Poppers
825	Smoked Eel	Orange Smoked Chicken	Tri-Tip Roast and Horseradish Chevre Crostini
826	Smoked Portobello Mushrooms with Herbs de Provence	Delicious Maple Glazed Smoked Bacon	Candied Bacon
827	Crazy Smoked Pork Spare Ribs	Smoked Volcano Potatoes	Chex Mix
828	Easy-Peasy Smoked Ribs	Tender Sweet Sriracha BBQ Chicken	Upside Down Cake
829	Supreme Chipotle Wings	Damn Feisty Pork Butt	Smoked Plums
830	Twice Pulled Potatoes	Honey Mustard Halibut Fillets	Plum Pie
831	Smoked "Onion Soup" Pork	Orange Crispy Chicken	Nutty Chocolate Bananas
832	Equally Worthy Cinnamon Cured Smoked Chicken	Slow Smoked Porterhouse Steaks	Bacon Wraps
833	Smoked Burgers	Smoked Fish in a Brine	Smoked Dessert Pizza
834	Authentic Citrus Smoked Chicken	Smoked Green Beans with Lemon	Beef Jerky
835	Simple Salt & Pepper Smoked Salmon	Smoked Ultimate Flank Steak	Venison Rolls
836	Basic Brisket	Amazing Mesquite Maple And Bacon Chicken	Hamburger Jerky
837	Memphis Style Beef Ribs	Herby Smoked Cauliflower	Smokey Pimento Cheese Appetizer
838	Smoked Summer Vegetables	Smoked Salmon	Sweet Tea Pork Jerky
839	Fully Smoked Herbal Quail	Slow Smoked Porterhouse Steaks	Pork Belly Burnt Ends
840	Smoked Steak Strips	Smoked Paprika Chicken	White Chocolate Bread Pudding
841	Smoked Fish with the Delicious Dip	Smoky Corn on the Cob	Roasted Pears
842	Smoked Lemony-Garlic Artichokes	Ultimate Chuck Roast	Smoke Roasted Apple Crisp
843	Sweet Cola Ribs	Classic Smoke Trout	Tangerine Smoked Flans

844	Honey Smoked Turkey	Smoked Squash Casserole	Smoked Peach Crumble
845	Pineapple Maple Glaze Fish In the Smoker	Curiously Smoked Italian Sausages	Baked Lemon Meringue Pie
846	Juicy Glaze Ham	Standing Smoked Chicken	Pork Tenderloin Appetizers
847	Smoked Potato Salad	Groovy smoked asparagus	Teriyaki Smoked Venison Jerky
848	Smoked Buffalo Chicken Wings	The Spacious Home Made Bacon	Summer Sausage
849	Strawberry and Jalapeno Smoked Ribs	Smoked Catfish Recipe	Stout Beef Jerky
850	Smoked Tuna	Smoked Eggplant	Jalapeno Poppers
851	Smoked Eel	Orange Smoked Chicken	Tri-Tip Roast and Horseradish Chevre Crostini
852	Smoked Portobello Mushrooms with Herbs de Provence	Delicious Maple Glazed Smoked Bacon	Candied Bacon
853	Crazy Smoked Pork Spare Ribs	Smoked Volcano Potatoes	Chex Mix
854	Easy-Peasy Smoked Ribs	Tender Sweet Sriracha BBQ Chicken	Upside Down Cake
855	Supreme Chipotle Wings	Damn Feisty Pork Butt	Smoked Plums
856	Twice Pulled Potatoes	Honey Mustard Halibut Fillets	Plum Pie
857	Smoked "Onion Soup" Pork	Orange Crispy Chicken	Nutty Chocolate Bananas
858	Equally Worthy Cinnamon Cured Smoked Chicken	Slow Smoked Porterhouse Steaks	Bacon Wraps
859	Smoked Burgers	Smoked Fish in a Brine	Smoked Dessert Pizza
860	Authentic Citrus Smoked Chicken	Smoked Green Beans with Lemon	Beef Jerky
861	Simple Salt & Pepper Smoked Salmon	Smoked Ultimate Flank Steak	Venison Rolls
862	Basic Brisket	Amazing Mesquite Maple And Bacon Chicken	Hamburger Jerky
863	Memphis Style Beef Ribs	Herby Smoked Cauliflower	Smokey Pimento Cheese Appetizer
864	Smoked Summer Vegetables	Smoked Salmon	Sweet Tea Pork Jerky
865	Fully Smoked Herbal Quail	Slow Smoked Porterhouse Steaks	Pork Belly Burnt Ends
866	Smoked Steak Strips	Smoked Paprika Chicken	White Chocolate Bread Pudding

867	Smoked Fish with the Delicious Dip	Smoky Corn on the Cob	Roasted Pears
868	Smoked Lemony-Garlic Artichokes	Ultimate Chuck Roast	Smoke Roasted Apple Crisp
869	Sweet Cola Ribs	Classic Smoke Trout	Tangerine Smoked Flans
870	Honey Smoked Turkey	Smoked Squash Casserole	Smoked Peach Crumble
871	Pineapple Maple Glaze Fish In the Smoker	Curiously Smoked Italian Sausages	Baked Lemon Meringue Pie
872	Juicy Glaze Ham	Standing Smoked Chicken	Pork Tenderloin Appetizers
873	Smoked Potato Salad	Groovy smoked asparagus	Teriyaki Smoked Venison Jerky
874	Smoked Buffalo Chicken Wings	The Spacious Home Made Bacon	Summer Sausage
875	Strawberry and Jalapeno Smoked Ribs	Smoked Catfish Recipe	Stout Beef Jerky
876	Smoked Tuna	Smoked Eggplant	Jalapeno Poppers
877	Smoked Eel	Orange Smoked Chicken	Tri-Tip Roast and Horseradish Chevre Crostini
878	Smoked Portobello Mushrooms with Herbs de Provence	Delicious Maple Glazed Smoked Bacon	Candied Bacon
879	Crazy Smoked Pork Spare Ribs	Smoked Volcano Potatoes	Chex Mix
880	Easy-Peasy Smoked Ribs	Tender Sweet Sriracha BBQ Chicken	Upside Down Cake
881	Supreme Chipotle Wings	Damn Feisty Pork Butt	Smoked Plums
882	Twice Pulled Potatoes	Honey Mustard Halibut Fillets	Plum Pie
883	Smoked "Onion Soup" Pork	Orange Crispy Chicken	Nutty Chocolate Bananas
884	Equally Worthy Cinnamon Cured Smoked Chicken	Slow Smoked Porterhouse Steaks	Bacon Wraps
885	Smoked Burgers	Smoked Fish in a Brine	Smoked Dessert Pizza
886	Authentic Citrus Smoked Chicken	Smoked Green Beans with Lemon	Beef Jerky
887	Simple Salt & Pepper Smoked Salmon	Smoked Ultimate Flank Steak	Venison Rolls
888	Basic Brisket	Amazing Mesquite Maple And Bacon Chicken	Hamburger Jerky
889	Memphis Style Beef Ribs	Herby Smoked Cauliflower	Smokey Pimento Cheese Appetizer

890	Smoked Summer Vegetables	Smoked Salmon	Sweet Tea Pork Jerky
891	Fully Smoked Herbal Quail	Slow Smoked Porterhouse Steaks	Pork Belly Burnt Ends
892	Smoked Steak Strips	Smoked Paprika Chicken	White Chocolate Bread Pudding
893	Smoked Fish with the Delicious Dip	Smoky Corn on the Cob	Roasted Pears
894	Smoked Lemony-Garlic Artichokes	Ultimate Chuck Roast	Smoke Roasted Apple Crisp
895	Sweet Cola Ribs	Classic Smoke Trout	Tangerine Smoked Flans
896	Honey Smoked Turkey	Smoked Squash Casserole	Smoked Peach Crumble
897	Pineapple Maple Glaze Fish In the Smoker	Curiously Smoked Italian Sausages	Baked Lemon Meringue Pie
898	Juicy Glaze Ham	Standing Smoked Chicken	Pork Tenderloin Appetizers
899	Smoked Potato Salad	Groovy smoked asparagus	Teriyaki Smoked Venison Jerky
900	Smoked Buffalo Chicken Wings	The Spacious Home Made Bacon	Summer Sausage
901	Strawberry and Jalapeno Smoked Ribs	Smoked Catfish Recipe	Stout Beef Jerky
902	Smoked Tuna	Smoked Eggplant	Jalapeno Poppers
903	Smoked Eel	Orange Smoked Chicken	Tri-Tip Roast and Horseradish Chevre Crostini
904	Smoked Portobello Mushrooms with Herbs de Provence	Delicious Maple Glazed Smoked Bacon	Candied Bacon
905	Crazy Smoked Pork Spare Ribs	Smoked Volcano Potatoes	Chex Mix
906	Easy-Peasy Smoked Ribs	Tender Sweet Sriracha BBQ Chicken	Upside Down Cake
907	Supreme Chipotle Wings	Damn Feisty Pork Butt	Smoked Plums
908	Twice Pulled Potatoes	Honey Mustard Halibut Fillets	Plum Pie
909	Smoked "Onion Soup" Pork	Orange Crispy Chicken	Nutty Chocolate Bananas
910	Equally Worthy Cinnamon Cured Smoked Chicken	Slow Smoked Porterhouse Steaks	Bacon Wraps
911	Smoked Burgers	Smoked Fish in a Brine	Smoked Dessert Pizza
912	Authentic Citrus Smoked Chicken	Smoked Green Beans with Lemon	Beef Jerky

913	Simple Salt & Pepper Smoked Salmon	Smoked Ultimate Flank Steak	Venison Rolls
914	Basic Brisket	Amazing Mesquite Maple And Bacon Chicken	Hamburger Jerky
915	Memphis Style Beef Ribs	Herby Smoked Cauliflower	Smokey Pimento Cheese Appetizer
916	Smoked Summer Vegetables	Smoked Salmon	Sweet Tea Pork Jerky
917	Fully Smoked Herbal Quail	Slow Smoked Porterhouse Steaks	Pork Belly Burnt Ends
918	Smoked Steak Strips	Smoked Paprika Chicken	White Chocolate Bread Pudding
919	Smoked Fish with the Delicious Dip	Smoky Corn on the Cob	Roasted Pears
920	Smoked Lemony-Garlic Artichokes	Ultimate Chuck Roast	Smoke Roasted Apple Crisp
921	Sweet Cola Ribs	Classic Smoke Trout	Tangerine Smoked Flans
922	Honey Smoked Turkey	Smoked Squash Casserole	Smoked Peach Crumble
923	Pineapple Maple Glaze Fish In the Smoker	Curiously Smoked Italian Sausages	Baked Lemon Meringue Pie
924	Juicy Glaze Ham	Standing Smoked Chicken	Pork Tenderloin Appetizers
925	Smoked Potato Salad	Groovy smoked asparagus	Teriyaki Smoked Venison Jerky
926	Smoked Buffalo Chicken Wings	The Spacious Home Made Bacon	Summer Sausage
927	Strawberry and Jalapeno Smoked Ribs	Smoked Catfish Recipe	Stout Beef Jerky
928	Smoked Tuna	Smoked Eggplant	Jalapeno Poppers
929	Smoked Eel	Orange Smoked Chicken	Tri-Tip Roast and Horseradish Chevre Crostini
930	Smoked Portobello Mushrooms with Herbs de Provence	Delicious Maple Glazed Smoked Bacon	Candied Bacon
931	Crazy Smoked Pork Spare Ribs	Smoked Volcano Potatoes	Chex Mix
932	Easy-Peasy Smoked Ribs	Tender Sweet Sriracha BBQ Chicken	Upside Down Cake
933	Supreme Chipotle Wings	Damn Feisty Pork Butt	Smoked Plums
934	Twice Pulled Potatoes	Honey Mustard Halibut Fillets	Plum Pie
935	Smoked "Onion Soup"	Orange Crispy Chicken	Nutty Chocolate

	Pork		Bananas
936	Equally Worthy Cinnamon Cured Smoked Chicken	Slow Smoked Porterhouse Steaks	Bacon Wraps
937	Smoked Burgers	Smoked Fish in a Brine	Smoked Dessert Pizza
938	Authentic Citrus Smoked Chicken	Smoked Green Beans with Lemon	Beef Jerky
939	Simple Salt & Pepper Smoked Salmon	Smoked Ultimate Flank Steak	Venison Rolls
940	Basic Brisket	Amazing Mesquite Maple And Bacon Chicken	Hamburger Jerky
941	Memphis Style Beef Ribs	Herby Smoked Cauliflower	Smokey Pimento Cheese Appetizer
942	Smoked Summer Vegetables	Smoked Salmon	Sweet Tea Pork Jerky
943	Fully Smoked Herbal Quail	Slow Smoked Porterhouse Steaks	Pork Belly Burnt Ends
944	Smoked Steak Strips	Smoked Paprika Chicken	White Chocolate Bread Pudding
945	Smoked Fish with the Delicious Dip	Smoky Corn on the Cob	Roasted Pears
946	Smoked Lemony-Garlic Artichokes	Ultimate Chuck Roast	Smoke Roasted Apple Crisp
947	Sweet Cola Ribs	Classic Smoke Trout	Tangerine Smoked Flans
948	Honey Smoked Turkey	Smoked Squash Casserole	Smoked Peach Crumble
949	Pineapple Maple Glaze Fish In the Smoker	Curiously Smoked Italian Sausages	Baked Lemon Meringue Pie
950	Juicy Glaze Ham	Standing Smoked Chicken	Pork Tenderloin Appetizers
951	Smoked Potato Salad	Groovy smoked asparagus	Teriyaki Smoked Venison Jerky
952	Smoked Buffalo Chicken Wings	The Spacious Home Made Bacon	Summer Sausage
953	Strawberry and Jalapeno Smoked Ribs	Smoked Catfish Recipe	Stout Beef Jerky
954	Smoked Tuna	Smoked Eggplant	Jalapeno Poppers
955	Smoked Eel	Orange Smoked Chicken	Tri-Tip Roast and Horseradish Chevre Crostini
956	Smoked Portobello Mushrooms with Herbs de Provence	Delicious Maple Glazed Smoked Bacon	Candied Bacon
957	Crazy Smoked Pork Spare Ribs	Smoked Volcano Potatoes	Chex Mix

958	Easy-Peasy Smoked Ribs	Tender Sweet Sriracha BBQ Chicken	Upside Down Cake
959	Supreme Chipotle Wings	Damn Feisty Pork Butt	Smoked Plums
960	Twice Pulled Potatoes	Honey Mustard Halibut Fillets	Plum Pie
961	Smoked "Onion Soup" Pork	Orange Crispy Chicken	Nutty Chocolate Bananas
962	Equally Worthy Cinnamon Cured Smoked Chicken	Slow Smoked Porterhouse Steaks	Bacon Wraps
963	Smoked Burgers	Smoked Fish in a Brine	Smoked Dessert Pizza
964	Authentic Citrus Smoked Chicken	Smoked Green Beans with Lemon	Beef Jerky
965	Simple Salt & Pepper Smoked Salmon	Smoked Ultimate Flank Steak	Venison Rolls
966	Basic Brisket	Amazing Mesquite Maple And Bacon Chicken	Hamburger Jerky
967	Memphis Style Beef Ribs	Herby Smoked Cauliflower	Smokey Pimento Cheese Appetizer
968	Smoked Summer Vegetables	Smoked Salmon	Sweet Tea Pork Jerky
969	Fully Smoked Herbal Quail	Slow Smoked Porterhouse Steaks	Pork Belly Burnt Ends
970	Smoked Steak Strips	Smoked Paprika Chicken	White Chocolate Bread Pudding
971	Smoked Fish with the Delicious Dip	Smoky Corn on the Cob	Roasted Pears
972	Smoked Lemony-Garlic Artichokes	Ultimate Chuck Roast	Smoke Roasted Apple Crisp
973	Sweet Cola Ribs	Classic Smoke Trout	Tangerine Smoked Flans
974	Honey Smoked Turkey	Smoked Squash Casserole	Smoked Peach Crumble
975	Pineapple Maple Glaze Fish In the Smoker	Curiously Smoked Italian Sausages	Baked Lemon Meringue Pie
976	Juicy Glaze Ham	Standing Smoked Chicken	Pork Tenderloin Appetizers
977	Smoked Potato Salad	Groovy smoked asparagus	Teriyaki Smoked Venison Jerky
978	Smoked Buffalo Chicken Wings	The Spacious Home Made Bacon	Summer Sausage
979	Strawberry and Jalapeno Smoked Ribs	Smoked Catfish Recipe	Stout Beef Jerky
980	Smoked Tuna	Smoked Eggplant	Jalapeno Poppers
981	Smoked Eel	Orange Smoked Chicken	Tri-Tip Roast and Horseradish Chevre

			Crostini
982	Smoked Portobello Mushrooms with Herbs de Provence	Delicious Maple Glazed Smoked Bacon	Candied Bacon
983	Crazy Smoked Pork Spare Ribs	Smoked Volcano Potatoes	Chex Mix
984	Easy-Peasy Smoked Ribs	Tender Sweet Sriracha BBQ Chicken	Upside Down Cake
985	Supreme Chipotle Wings	Damn Feisty Pork Butt	Smoked Plums
986	Twice Pulled Potatoes	Honey Mustard Halibut Fillets	Plum Pie
987	Smoked "Onion Soup" Pork	Orange Crispy Chicken	Nutty Chocolate Bananas
988	Equally Worthy Cinnamon Cured Smoked Chicken	Slow Smoked Porterhouse Steaks	Bacon Wraps
989	Smoked Burgers	Smoked Fish in a Brine	Smoked Dessert Pizza
990	Authentic Citrus Smoked Chicken	Smoked Green Beans with Lemon	Beef Jerky
991	Simple Salt & Pepper Smoked Salmon	Smoked Ultimate Flank Steak	Venison Rolls
992	Basic Brisket	Amazing Mesquite Maple And Bacon Chicken	Hamburger Jerky
993	Memphis Style Beef Ribs	Herby Smoked Cauliflower	Smokey Pimento Cheese Appetizer
994	Smoked Summer Vegetables	Smoked Salmon	Sweet Tea Pork Jerky
995	Fully Smoked Herbal Quail	Slow Smoked Porterhouse Steaks	Pork Belly Burnt Ends
996	Smoked Steak Strips	Smoked Paprika Chicken	White Chocolate Bread Pudding
997	Smoked Fish with the Delicious Dip	Smoky Corn on the Cob	Roasted Pears
998	Smoked Lemony-Garlic Artichokes	Ultimate Chuck Roast	Smoke Roasted Apple Crisp
999	Sweet Cola Ribs	Classic Smoke Trout	Tangerine Smoked Flans
1000	Honey Smoked Turkey	Smoked Squash Casserole	Smoked Peach Crumble

CONCLUSION

Thanks for downloading this book. Are you an experienced pit master or is this your very first smoker purchase? If you've smoked food a lot in the past, you have a good idea of how long foods take, how they look when they're done, how hot a smoker needs to be, and so on. You would be more comfortable using an analog electric smoker than someone who is very new at the smoking game. Beginners tend to prefer the exact temperature precision of digital electric smokers and are willing to pay more for that control. Think about your experience with BBQ when selecting a smoker and you'll find one designed with you in mind.

Different parts of a smoker might need to be replaced at different times, like the smoker racks in two to three years. Generally, good smokers should last at least five years. Their longevity depends on how often you use yours and how often and how well you clean it.

All that said, I hope you enjoy the recipes covered herein. Thank you.

All the best!!

Made in the USA
Coppell, TX
15 March 2020

16895075R00108